Design for Six Sigma^{+Lean} Toolset

Stephan Lunau (Ed.)

Christian Staudter
Jens-Peter Mollenhauer
Renata Meran
Olin Roenpage
Clemens von Hugo
Alexis Hamalides

Design for Six Sigma +Lean Toolset

Implementing Innovations Successfully

 Springer

Editor:
Dipl.-Kfm. Stephan Lunau
UMS GmbH Consulting
Hanauer Landstraße 291B
60314 Frankfurt
Germany
stephan.lunau@ums.gmbh.com

Authors:
Dipl.-Bw. Christian Staudter
Dipl.-Wirt.-Ing., Dipl.-Ing. Jens-Peter Mollenhauer
Dipl.-Vw. Renata Meran
Mag. Olin Roenpage
Clemens von Hugo
Dipl.-Wirt.-Ing. Alexis Hamalides

UMS GmbH Consulting
Hanauer Landstraße 291B
60314 Frankfurt
Germany

ISBN 978-3-540-89513-8   e-ISBN 978-3-540-89514-5

DOI 10.1007/978-3-540-89514-5

Library of Congress Control Number: 2008940146

Cover design: WMXDesign GmbH, Heidelberg, Germany

Printed on acid-free paper

9 8 7 6 5 4 3 2 1

springer.com

Table of Contents

Contents

Contents

Contents

Contents

Foreword

Every company relies on innovation to compete globally. However, creative ideas are mostly insufficient if you want to translate an innovative spirit into commercial success. The ability to put a new product or a new process on the market as quickly as possible is becoming increasingly important.
Systematic management is necessary for developing cost-effective and successful products based on market realities and customer requirements. Especially open innovation, which is currently intensively discussed and widely implemented, requires consideration. Only a sensible interface and information management is capable of generating overall success from a variety of good ideas.

Design for Six Sigma^{+Lean} is an approach for such a systematic innovation management. This concept was developed to achieve a target-oriented realization of innovations and is strongly associated with the Six Sigma^{+Lean} methodology, currently applied globally to optimize existing processes. DFSS^{+Lean} synthesizes a number of key factors, including the active integration of employees, customer-oriented development, the reduction of complexity in products and processes, and controlling of innovation in terms of a standardized procedure.

The present toolset represents the proven approach UMS takes when putting Design for Six Sigma^{+Lean} into practice. Its individual tools are assigned to the process model Define, Measure, Analyze, Design, and Verify in a clear and manageable structure. This structure can be considered as a red thread and makes it easier to apply the tools in practice and organize an innovative product and process development that is target-oriented and efficient.

Besides the whole UMS team, I would like to thank the authors, who along with their expertise and experience have shown enormous commitment in putting this book together. My thanks also go to Mariana Winterhager for the graphic layout of the material and Astrid Schmitz for the translation work.

I wish everyone great success in implementing innovations.

Frankfurt am Main, October 2008

Stephan Lunau

Design for Six Sigma^{+Lean} Toolset

Introduction

Introduction

Content:

Implementing innovation successfully

The Six Sigma^{+Lean} Approach
- The goal of Six Sigma^{+Lean}
- The four dimensions of Six Sigma^{+Lean}

Developing new processes and / or products with DFSS^{+Lean}

Critical Success Factors
- Employee acceptance
- The quality of the applied tools and methods

Summary: Benefits of DFSS^{+Lean}

Implementing Innovation Successfully

Today innovation is one of the most important success factors for every company: according to an up-to-date benchmark study conducted by the American Productivity and Quality Control (APQC)*, companies displaying strong growth generate one-third of their turnover from products which are younger than three years. A further key observation: over the last 50 years the lifecycles of new products have shortened by 400% on average. Successful innovation is obviously not only due to good ideas, but requires quick implementation.
But the implementation step includes great difficulties for many companies: statistics show that from 100 R&D projects only every tenth generates commercial success and even an on-schedule market launch is met by only every second product.

Every innovation demands from companies a balancing act between customer requirements and internal effort/expenditure and the risks. On the one hand customer requirements are to be met exactly (effectiveness), while on the other hand low costs and a quick introduction to the market (efficiency) are to be realized.

Two sides of the coin

Efficiency:
*Lowering costs –
ensuring competitiveness*

Effectiveness:
*Complete fulfillment
of customer requirements –
strategic creation of the
markets of tomorrow*

The question is: how is a balance to be achieved between the benefits for the customer and the effort/expenditure for the company?

Implementing innovation successfully thus means making a good idea marketable in the shortest possible time while the risk for the company is minimized at the same time. This can only be achieved through systematic management of developmental work.

---

* *American Productivity & Quality Center (2003): Improving New Product Development Performance and Practices. Houston (TX): APQC (www.apqc.org/pubs/NPD2003)*

Such an innovation management must avoid the risks typical of product development. These are:
- Customer requirements are either not identified at all or only insufficiently; products/services unsuitable for the market are thus developed.
- Resources are deployed in line with false priorities (waste of resources).
- Features are added to products/services, which the customers don't want (Overengineering).
- Only a few members of the development team determine the process.
- Project results are not completely documented and are not understandable.
- The introduction to the market is delayed (time to market) through unplanned and time-consuming rework.

Innovation management must also be able to respond flexibly to the individual requirements of different project types.

Project Type / Project-Characteristics	Breakthrough Innovation	Mixed Types	Incremental Improvement
Complexity	High		Low
Degree of Novelty	High		Low
Variability	High		Low
Degree of Structuring	Low		High

DFSS can be used for all project types. The deployment of specific methods and tools must be calibrated and coordinated to match the respective development task. However, the logical structure remains the same.
With Design for Six Sigma (DFSS[+Lean]) an approach has been put into practice worldwide and across many sectors in recent years that is capable of successfully implementing these requirements.

6

Through a structured combination of proven methods and tools from the Six Sigma, Lean Management, and system development environment, DFSS[+Lean] offers the possibility to systematically and efficiently boost innovation in the company.

The description of the development process in terms of the DMADV phase cycle (DMADV = Define, Measure, Analyze, Design, Verify) makes it possible to apply DFSS[+Lean] to different innovation levels and to support process and product development in equal measure.

DMADV provides methodological support on three of five innovation levels.

Innovation Levels	Application Areas	Methods
1	Process optimization	DMAIC: elimination of negative quality
2	Development of a new product based on an existing process (in line with changes in the market)	DMADV: generation of positive quality
3	Development of a new process to further develop an existing product (e.g. during production transfers)	
4	Development of a new product and a new process	
5	Basic research	

The risk of misguided development or "never ending stories" is reduced significantly. Successes become repeatable.

Example on the following page.

Successes become repeatable with DFSS^{+Lean}

- Customer interaction with the product or the process is studied intensively – the genuine requirements of the target customers form the starting point
- The whole value chain from the idea to further development is taken into consideration
- All functions are covered by the core development team
- Resources are deployed in a target-oriented way
- Clearly defined phase sections and contents structure development work
- Customers are encouraged to provide feedback at given times
- Results are documented in line with a standard form

Design For Six Sigma^{+Lean} is a key element of the Six Sigma^{+Lean} concept and pursues the same approach. This will be briefly presented on the following pages.

The Six Sigma+Lean Approach

Six Sigma+Lean is the systematic further development and combination of proven tools and methods for improving processes. Emphasis is placed on the consistent orientation to customer requirements and a concept of quality that integrates the "benefit" for the stakeholders.

Six Sigma+Lean derives the elimination of defects and waste from a systematic analysis of processes based on facts. Implementing an integrative measurement and project systematic achieves a lasting increase in both customer satisfaction and company value. The concept mobilizes and demands the commitment of all executives and thus, when applied consistently, provides an integrated approach for changing the entire company culture.

Six Sigma+Lean is applicable in every industry and service branch and is broadly accepted on capital and labor markets.
Because of that this method also has a positive influence on the image and shareholder value of a company.

The Goal of Six Sigma+Lean

Six Sigma+Lean shows that the demand to enhance quality while reducing costs at the same time must not represent a contradiction.
If quality is determined in relation to customers, every increase in quality represents added value that the customer is prepared to pay for.
The goal of every Six Sigma+Lean project is therefore: to achieve perceivable quality through marketable products while significantly cutting costs through lean processes.

This special approach forms the basis of the special Six Sigma+Lean vision of quality, which has as its goal the benefit generated for both the customer as well as the company:

To meet
customer requirements
fully and profitably.

The Four Dimensions of Six Sigma^{+Lean}

Six Sigma^{+Lean} comprises four key elements or dimensions in order to realize this vision:

- The iterative cycle employed to optimize processes, called the DMAIC, that consists of the five phases, **D**efine, **M**easure, **A**nalyze, **I**mprove, and **C**ontrol
- The procedural model for developing processes and products, called the DMADV, that consists of the five phases, **D**efine, **M**easure, **A**nalyze, **D**esign, and **V**erify (also known as DFSS, Design for Six Sigma)
- Lean Tools applied in the two aforementioned approaches
- Process Management for ensuring sustainability

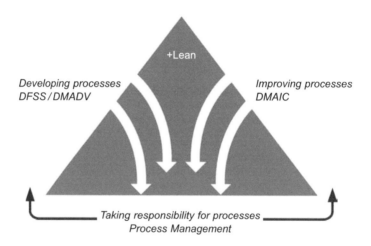

With DMAIC, Six Sigma^{+Lean} has at its disposal tools and methods for improving products or processes, while the DMADV cycle provides an approach enabling the developedment of new products and processes.

Generating well-founded results, the DMAIC iterative cycle represents the basis for a systematic project work which is based on facts. The key goal of this improvement methodology is to decrease process lead times by reducing rework, waste, and inventories. Existing potential is realized by systematically eliminating errors and defects.

The procedural model DMADV or DFSS⁺ᴸᵉᵃⁿ aims at satisfying customer needs. Based on systematic surveys new products and processes are developed which create value for the customer. The framework for developmental work is set by the following customer values.

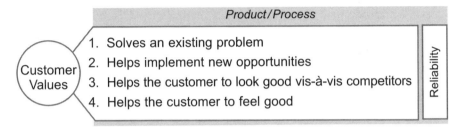

The combination of both approaches in Six Sigma⁺ᴸᵉᵃⁿ matches the insight that:

"Not doing anything wrong doesn't mean that one is doing everything right!"

This is because: DMAIC lastingly eliminates negative quality, while with DFSS⁺ᴸᵉᵃⁿ new positive quality can be generated.

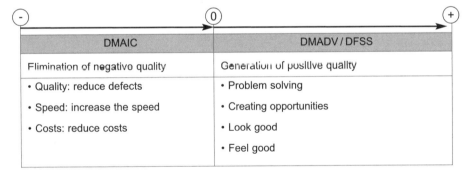

DMAIC	DMADV / DFSS
Elimination of negative quality	Generation of positive quality
• Quality: reduce defects	• Problem solving
• Speed: increase the speed	• Creating opportunities
• Costs: reduce costs	• Look good
	• Feel good

Both approaches complement one another during Six Sigma⁺ᴸᵉᵃⁿ project work, so that a launched DMAIC project can at several places in the cycle be converted into or induce a DMADV/DFSS⁺ᴸᵉᵃⁿ project.

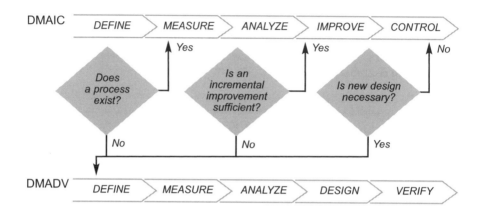

Developing New Processes and/or Products with DFSS+Lean

DFSS projects concentrate on generating value for the respective target customers. A perceivable value always arises when a product/process exactly fulfills customer needs.

One necessary prerequisite for developing "valuable" products and processes is therefore the systematic identification of customer requirements. When weighted and prioritized they – and not the preferences of the developers – function as the motor of the project.
In addition, they facilitate the concentration on limited resources.

On this basis the DMADV procedural plan sketched below is suitable for the development of follow-up products and the elaboration of completely new products or processes.

Phases	DMADV Procedural Plan
DEFINE	• Business case • Project planning and scoping
MEASURE	• Understanding customer requirements • Transformation into specific and measurable customor requirements • Deriving target values and tolerances
ANALYZE	• Development of an optimal high-level design concept
DESIGN	• Elaboration of the design down to the smallest detail • Production and implementation planning
VERIFY	• Pilot and/or test • Complete implementation • Monitoring the KPIs

Proven tools and methods from the Six Sigma, Lean Management, and System Development environment are deployed in each phase of this DMADV cycle:

	Tools	Goal
Define	• Project Charter • Project Scope • Multigeneration Plan (MGP) • Gantt Chart • RACI Chart • Budget Calculation • Stakeholder Analysis Table • Communication Plan • Risk Analysis	• The project is defined. • Problem and goal are defined and complemented by a MGP. • The project is clearly scoped and its influence on other projects reviewed. • Activity, time, and resource planning is defined. • Possible project risks are identified and assessed.
Measure	• Portfolio Analysis • Kano Model • Customer Interaction Study • Survey Techniques • Affinity Diagram • Tree Diagram • Benchmarking • House of Quality • Design Scorecards	• The relevant customers are identified and segmented. • Customer requirements are collected, sorted, and prioritized. • CTQs and measurements are derived on the basis of customer requirements. • For measurements priorities are allotted, target values and quality key figures defined.
Analyze	• Function Analysis • Transfer Function • QFD 2 • Creativity Techniques • Ishikawa Diagram • TRIZ • Benchmarking • Pugh Matrix • FMEA • Anticipated Defect Detection • Design Scorecards • Process Modeling • Prototyping	• The best concept is selected from alternative high-level concepts. • Conflicts and contradictions in the selected concept are solved and the necessary resources are derived. • The remaining risk is defined, customer feedback is gathered, and the concept is finalized.

Tools	Goal
Design • QFD 3 • Statistical Methods (Tolerancing, Hypothesis Tests, DOE) • Design Scorecards • FMEA • QFD 4 • Radar Chart • Lean Toolbox (Value Stream Design, Pull Systems, SMED, Lot Sizing, Complexity, Poka Yoke, Process Balancing)	• The detailed concept is developed, optimized, and evaluated. • The production process is planned and optimized in line with Lean principles. • The implementation of the process design is prepared, involved employees are informed, and customer feedback was gathered.
Verify • PDCA Cycle • Project Management • Training • SOPs	• The Pilot is carried out, analyzed, and the Roll Out planned. • The production process is implemented. • The process is handed over completely to the Process Owner, the documentation was passed on, and the project completed.

The correct use of these methods and tools contributes significantly to a successful DFSS project.

Critical Success Factors

Along with the quality of the deployed methods and tools, the success of a DFSS project also depends to a great extent on the acceptance within the company.

[SUCCESS] (=)	[ACCEPTANCE] (x)	[QUALITY]
Innovative new and/or further development of products and services trimmed exactly to meet requirements which can be sold to a sufficiently large pool of customers in a profitable way	• Interdisciplinary team with changing responsibilities during different phases • Disciplined project management in the frame of Six Sigma roles and responsibilities, applying DFSS^{+Lean} tools • Specific and measurable criteria to regulate the preparatory and specific work of all divisions involved in the development process • Risk management to evaluate the project environment • Active stakeholder management during the project course	• Offer the customer "valuable" products and services, i. e. identify, understand, and translate customer needs • Coherency and coordination • Innovate new and/or further development to solve problems in such a way that the customer benefits and benefit/value is generated • "Quality" as stringent orientation for company performance to customer requirements

Employee Acceptance

A successful implementation of the DFSS project contributes more than anything else to ensuring acceptance.

Forming an interdisciplinary team creates a platform covering many areas and functions. This platform enables the efficient fulfillment of the development task which is achieved by applying common tools and methods. Defects, double work, and loops are avoided, while project criteria are met more easily. The joint project work establishes a common language understood by everyone and thus improves communication across all areas.

Usually a DFSS team is made up of employees from the following areas, or is at least supported by them:

The defined team is accompanied by an internal/external coach who introduces the necessary methods and tools in the course of development work and applies them while working with the team. In this way the employees from the various areas extend their methodological skills with proven tools and methods. The learnt success becomes repeatable.

The DFSS[+Lean] investment in human capital is thus goal-oriented and sustainable. The resultant distinctive profiles of companies applying these methods vis-à-vis their competitors cannot be offset by gaining the services of "knowing" employees.

Besides an interdisciplinary core team, the acceptance of the DFSS[+Lean] project is promoted in the company by a number of other factors:
- Management commitment
- Providing suitable resources with sufficient know-how and prompt availability
- Team ability of the core team
- Systematic application of tools and methods
- Creativity
- Integration of DFSS tools and methods into existing development processes
- Defining and sticking to the project profile/scope
- Goal-oriented and systematic project management

The Quality of Applied Tools and Methods

In line with the success story of Six Sigma in process optimization (DMAIC), the success of the DFSS[+Lean] concept is not based on inventing new tools and methods. On the contrary: many of the methods and tools dealt with in this toolset have proven worthwhile for a number of years in meeting the challenges of development processes. Crucial to the success of the DFSS concept is how these tools and methods are combined with one another.

A further success factor of the DFSS[+Lean] approach is its integrated perspective of the product life cycle, from the idea to the utilization of the obsolete product under the systematic consideration of financial key figures.

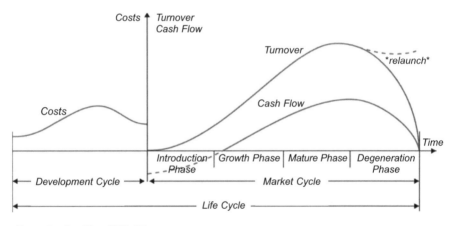

Diagram from Bea / Haas (1997): 113

A sensible combination of the Six Sigma[+Lean] toolsets DMAIC, DFSS, and Lean Management provides quick, goal-oriented solutions for the most complex problems and ensures a flexible and customer-oriented further development of the respective product/process. The successful implementation of the tools is secured through the company's well-trained employees.

Whoever has to reach a decision on the use of a DFSS[+Lean] approach in operative practice should consider the following aspect:

In our practical experience of DFSS^{+Lean} UMS has repeatedly observed how advantageous it is to integrate the concept into an already existing development process. In this context the quality of the deployed aids can develop its optimal potential and so guarantee the acceptance of the participating employees.

Summary: the Benefits of DFSS⁺ᴸᵉᵃⁿ

Because the goal of the DFSS⁺ᴸᵉᵃⁿ approach is to meet the requirements of both the customer and the company, it generates a diverse array of benefits for everyone involved in the development process:

Contents	Company	Employee/Team
• Perceivable benefit (value) • Products/processes and systems in line with requirements • Reliable products/processes and systems • Good cost-benefit ratio	• Security and risk minimization • Short time-to-market • Service and repair cost minimization • Margin security through USP • Enhanced image • Repeatable successes	• Effective tools • Common language • Security in every phase of the project (flow-up/flow-down) • Repeatable successes • Greater motivation

Design for Six Sigma^{+Lean} Toolset

DEFINE

DEFINE

MEASURE

ANALYZE

DESIGN

VERIFY

Phase 1: Define

Goals

- – Initiating the project
- – Determining project scope and management
- – Setting project goals

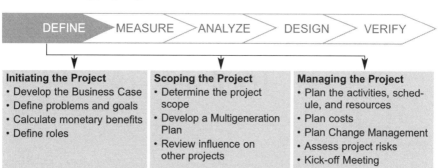

Initiating the Project	Scoping the Project	Managing the Project
• Develop the Business Case	• Determine the project scope	• Plan the activities, schedule, and resources
• Define problems and goals	• Develop a Multigeneration Plan	• Plan costs
• Calculate monetary benefits	• Review influence on other projects	• Plan Change Management
• Define roles		• Assess project risks
		• Kick-off Meeting

Approach

A DFSS project is defined in such a way that it fits in with the overall company strategy.

A roadmap for the Define Phase is presented on the opposite page.

Most Important Tools

- • Project Charter
- • Project Framework, Project Scoping
- • Multigeneration Plan (MGP)
- • Gantt Chart
- • RACI Chart
- • Budget Calculation, Cost Planning
- • Communication Plan, Change Management
- • Stakeholder Analysis Table
- • Risk Analysis and Assessment

Define Roadmap

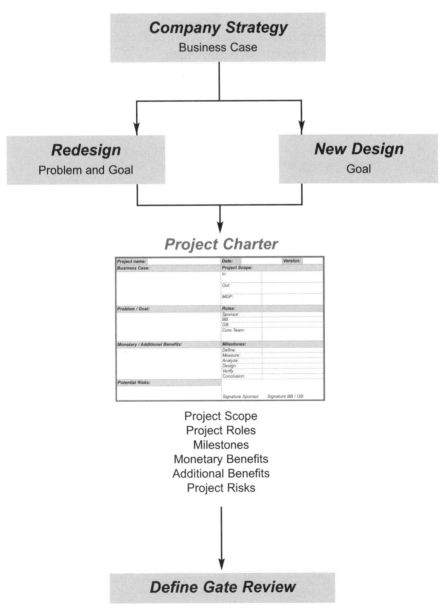

DEFINE

MEASURE

ANALYZE

DESIGN

VERIFY

DEFINE

MEASURE

ANALYZE

DESIGN

VERIFY

Project Charter

📁 **Term / Description**
Project Charter, Project Order, Project Profile

🕐 **When**
In the Define Phase, validated in all subsequent phases: Measure, Analyze, Design, Verify

◎ **Goal**
Summarize all information necessary for defining the project

▶▶ **Steps**
A Project Charter is the key document of the Define Phase. It summarizes all the important information for launching the project by using the following elements:

Elements of a Project Charter

Initiating the Project	**1.**	**Business Case** Explanatory statement of why the project should be carried out now
	2.a	**Redesign: Problems and Goals** Description of problems / chances as well as the goals in clear, concise, and measurable terms
	2.b	**New Design: Goal** Naming a new product / process and its terms of reference and goals
	3.	**Project Benefits** Financial benefits generated by the project and, if applicable, non-quantifiable soft savings
	4.	**Roles** Sponsor, Black Belt, Green Belt, Team Members, Master Black Belt
Scoping the Project	**5.**	**Project Boundaries** What is "in" and "out", Multigeneration Plan (MGP)
Managing the Project	**6.**	**Project Management** Main steps and milestones for achieving goals, project risks

DEFINE

The Sponsor is responsible for drawing up a provisional Project Charter. The contents are discussed and coordinated with management, the Deployment Champion, marketing, sales, and the Black Belts / Green Belts.

Project Charter

Example: passenger seat

MEASURE

Project name:	Development of a passenger seat for Russia	Date:	August 17, 2007	Version:	D1
Business Case:		**Project Scope:**			
Market studies have shown that transport companies in Russia plan to modernize their bus fleets by up to 80% over the next 10 years. To meet this demand a new passenger seat is to be developed on the basis of customer requirements.		*In:*	Passenger seat, installation & removal, variability of interior, laws, standards		
		Out:	Electronic features, massage function		
		MGP:	Generation I: 30% market share in Russia by 2007, modular standard fitting		
Problem / Goal:		**Roles:**			
Development and product launch of a new, robust passenger seat for Russian transport companies by December 23, 2007 at the latest. The bus manufacturers and suppliers in Western Europe are to be actively involved in the development process.		*Sponsor:*	Dr. Jacomo Franco		
		BB:	Bernhard Fuchsberger		
		GB:			
		Core Team:	Ms. M. (Marketing), Dr. Q. (Quality Management), Dr. F. (R & D), Mr. E. (Procurement), Ms. P. (Production), Dr. V. (Sales)		
Monetary / Additional Benefits:		**Milestones:**			
Output 2005: 20,000; 2006: 30,000; 2007: 50,000 Profit per seat = 10% of net sale price, net sale price = €100, tax rate = 25%; capital cost rate = 10%, → EVA 2005 = €150,000, EVA 2006 = €225,000, EVA 2007 = €375,000, discounted EVA on 2005 = €664,500.		*Define:*	August 17, 2007		
		Measure:	September 10, 2007		
		Analyze:	October 8, 2007		
		Design:	November 5, 2007		
		Verify:	December 3, 2007		
		Conclusion:	December 23, 2007		
Potential Risks:					
Increased political intervention in the Russian domestic market, possible liquidity problems amongst the trading partners, logistics and transport of the product in Russia.		*Signature Sponsor*		*Signature BB / GB*	

ANALYZE

DESIGN

VERIFY

Business Case

📁 **Term / Description**

Business Case, depicting the starting situation

🕐 **When**

In the Define Phase, validated in all subsequent phases: Measure, Analyze, Design, Verify

◎ **Goals**

– Describe the business environment and the starting situation
– Describe the importance and impact of the project for customers and the company

▶▶ **Steps**

Developing the Business Case requires finding the answers to the following questions:

– Provisional market and competition analysis:
  - describing target market and target customer
  - provisional customer needs and / or requirements
  - benefits for the customer / market potential
  - competition analysis / benchmarking
  - benefits for the company / turnover potential
– Why shall the project be carried out now?
– Are there any other projects in the company which are dealing with this or similar topics?
– Which other projects are being treated with the same priority?
– Does the goal of this project conform to company strategies and mid-term goals?
– What benefit does this project have for the company?

These questions are clarified through the active input of the following:

– *Deployment Champion* (company strategies),
– *Marketing and Sales* (forecasts on target market, customer, and competitive strategies),

– *Management and senior employees,*
– *Black and Green Belts and potential team members, who contribute their specialist know-how.*

⇨ **Tips**

• Based on facts and easily understandable, the Business Case is to show management and stakeholders the background and context of the project.
• It is therefore important at this point to convey the need for action!
• For more detailed information on drawing up a Business Case or a Business Plan consult the listed economics literature.

DEFINE

MEASURE

ANALYZE

DESIGN

VERIFY

27

DEFINE

MEASURE

ANALYZE

DESIGN

VERIFY

Redesign

☐ **Term / Description**
Redesign Order, depicting the problem and goal

🕐 **When**
In the Define Phase, initiating the project

◎ **Goal**
Describe the problem and the improvements aimed at

▸▸ **Steps**
Redesign must first of all clearly depict the problem. Answering the following questions generates a good supportive basis for describing the problem:
   – What is going wrong or does not match customer requirements?
   – When and where do the problems occur?
   – How big are the problems?
   – What are the effects of the problems?
   – Can the team collect data to quantify and analyze the problems?
   – Why can the improvement not be achieved without redesign?

A clear goal can only be formulated after precisely depicting the problem. This goal must be measurable and must include a conclusion date. If the project addresses more than one problem, accordingly several goals must be formulated.

⇒ **Tips**
Pay close attention to the SMART rule:
   • Specific
   • Measureable
   • Agreed to
   • Realistic
   • Time bound

DEFINE

Many project launches even fail to get off the ground due to imprecise problem descriptions and goal formulations. An objective description of actual and target states is necessary.
Therefore:
At this point no description of causes, no formulation of solutions, and no blaming!

MEASURE

ANALYZE

DESIGN

VERIFY

DEFINE

MEASURE

ANALYZE

DESIGN

VERIFY

New Design

📂 **Term / Description**

New Design, development of a new product / service / process

🕓 **When**

In the Define Phase, initiating the project

◎ **Goal**

Describe the new product or service idea and the chances it presents (when no redesign is present)

▸▸ **Steps**

The development goal must be measurable and must contain a concluding date.

⇨ **Tips**

Pay close attention to the SMART rule:

- Specific
- Measureable
- Agreed to
- Realistic
- Time bound

Many project launches even fail to get off the ground due to imprecise problem descriptions and goal formulations. An objective description of actual and target states is necessary.

Therefore:

At this point no description of causes, no formulation of solutions, and no blaming!

30

Project Benefit

📋 **Term / Description**
Project Benefit, hard and soft savings

🕑 **When**
In the Define Phase, validated in all subsequent phases: Measure, Analyze, Design, Verify

◎ **Goal**
Evaluate the quantitative and qualitative project benefit for the company

▶▶ **Steps**
Development projects aim at supporting the company strategy and thus positively influencing the key performance indicators according to which a company is managed.

The benefit of a development project is evaluated by the Sponsor with the help of the Business Case and verified with an employee from Controlling. The project benefit is derived from the difference between the actual state (problem / chance / idea) and target state (goal) and expressed as viable earning power.

The EVA® (Economic Value Added) is a financial performance indicator that describes the profit generated surplus to capital costs. It is included in the following observations so as to show the monetary effects of DFSS projects. *(An example of EVA® is given on the following page.)*

The value drivers depicted also impact on other key financial figures, e.g. ROI, cash flow, EBIDTA, which are used to steer and control operations in accordance with the specific company profile.

Apart from the monetary benefit, the project often includes unquantifiable successes, so-called soft savings. These should also be considered and described.

DEFINE

MEASURE

ANALYZE

DESIGN

VERIFY

Classical soft savings are for example:
- – Enhancement of prestige through excellent quality,
- – Level of awareness of the brand or company,
- – Increased employee motivation and retention of High Potentials to the company,
- – Better security at the workplace (safety first).

EVA® Example – Value Drivers

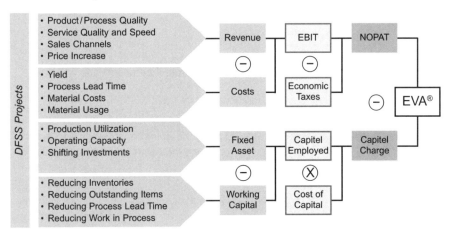

EVA® *is a registered brand of the business consultancy Stern Stewart & Co.*

Project Team

📁 **Term/Description**
Project Team, Core Team, Task Force

🕐 **When**
In the Define Phase, initiating the project

◎ **Goal**
Define a core team for the project capable of action

▶▶ **Steps**
A key factor of successful DFSS projects is an interdisciplinary core team that consists of members taken from as many areas of the involved value chain as possible:
– Marketing,
– Sales,
– Research & Development,
– Production,
– Quality Management,
– Customer Services.

Before the project starts, the Project Leader should consider in consultation with the team who is required, when he is required, and what responsibility each member is given.
It is advisable to go on the offensive and make concrete proposals to the Sponsor.
The Sponsor is then responsible for ensuring that the capacities agreed to are put at the disposal of the core team.
It is important at the kick-off meeting to make the team members aware of how responsibility shifts over the course of the project from Marketing/Sales through to R&D to Production and Quality Management *(cf. RACI Chart)*.

Project Scope

☐ Term / Description
In-Out-Frame, Project Scope

⊙ When
In the Define Phase, validated in all subsequent phases: Measure, Analyze, Design, Verify

◎ Goals
– Focus the project on coordinated contents
– Clearly determine those issues and topics which are not part of the project
– Visually assign the different aspects
– Guarantee a common understanding of the product or process

▶▶ Steps
The following questions are helpful for scoping a project:
– Which product / process should the team concentrate on?
– Which issues are not to be addressed within this project?
– How is this product marked off from other products / product families?
– Is there any overlapping with other projects and how are they to be prioritized?
– What is the future vision for the product / process?

The Project Scope is visualized as a frame. All aspects affecting the project are positioned within the frame.
The issues the team needs to consider are placed inside the frame.
The issues which do not need to be considered in this project are positioned outside the frame.
The issues which cannot be conclusively assigned to either "in" or "out" are positioned on the frame. The team is to discuss their final positioning. If no clear decision can be made, the Sponsor is to be consulted.

In-Out-Frame
Example: passenger seat

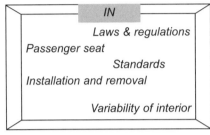

IN
- Laws & regulations
- Passenger seat
- Standards
- Installation and removal
- Variability of interior

OUT
- Electronics fitted to seat
- Massage function
- Changes to the bus layout

Project Frame

Multigeneration Plan, MGP

📁 **Term / Description**
Multigeneration Plan, MGP

🕐 **When**
In the Define Phase, to be considered in all subsequent phases: Measure, Analyze, Design, Verify

◎ **Goals**
– Focus on specific contents in a development project
– Support long-term planning
– Gain a perspective on the future development of the system (product / process)

▶▶ **Steps**
The Multigeneration Plan describes the system development on the basis of three generations, each of which builds on its predecessor.

Example of a Multigeneration Plan

Generation I	Generation II	Generation III
Take the first step! Generation I aims at eliminating urgent problems and filling gaps Stop the bleeding!	Improve the position gained! Generation II extends a secured product basis and is devoted to offensively opening up new target markets. Take the offensive!	Generation III strives for a quantum leap with sweeping success, e.g. becoming "technological market leader". Attain leadership!
Stop the bleeding!	Take the offensive!	Attain leadership!

Time elapsed →

36

Each generation is described by
- its vision / its goal,
- its characteristic features,
- the technologies and platforms required.

The time set for the system is based on how the market and competitors develop.

⇨ **Tips**

Other orientation points are:
- Processes and systems which are important for achieving more efficient and quicker developments and bringing products onto the market.
- Sales and distribution channels and structures which place the product in its assigned target market.

Multigeneration Plan

Example: passenger seat

	Generation I	*Generation II*	*Generation III*
Vision / Goal	Passenger seat for the "rural market" in Russia, market share 30%	Passenger seat for the "rural market" in Eastern Europe, market share 40%	Passenger seat for the "rural market" worldwide, market share 50%
System Generation	Based on customer requirements In Russia, modular standard fitting	Extension of standard fitting based on new customer requirements if required	Enhancing complexity in line with local conditions
Platforms and Technologies	Existing processes and technologies, low investments, a further offer on the website, catalogue...	Extension of sales and service processes, support through B2B-E-Business applications	Expanding production and locating it to other countries

DEFINE

MEASURE

ANALYZE

DESIGN

VERIFY

37

DEFINE

MEASURE

ANALYZE

DESIGN

VERIFY

Project Mapping

☐ Term/Description

Project Mapping, evaluating the influence on other projects, project overview

◔ When

In the Define Phase, with validation in all subsequent phases: Measure, Analyze, Design, Verify

◎ Goals

- Evaluate the mutual influence between the DFSS project and other projects in the company
- Secure an effective and efficient exchange of information

►► Steps

The following questions are helpful when evaluating the influence of other projects:

Internal projects

- Can the DFSS project use information generated by other projects being carried out in the company at the same time?
- Can other projects use the DFSS project's information and interim results?
- Do other projects influence the DFSS project in terms of expected constraints in the resources for the test environment, production, marketing, procurement, sales?
- What is the best way to document and communicate information to ensure effective and efficient information exchange between employees involved in the different projects?

External projects

- What projects are your competitors currently involved in?
- What projects or initiatives are being carried out by the customer?
- Are regulatory changes to be expected during the course of the project?

Project Mapping
Example: passenger seat

Projects to be considered	
External	*Internal*
New developments by competitors	Project Single sourcing (procurement)
Optimization initiatives by customers	Project Optimizing spray-painting process
EU initiative on fire protection in passenger buses	Project Restructuring

39

DEFINE

MEASURE

ANALYZE

DESIGN

VERIFY

Project Management

☐ Term / Description
Project Management, planning, monitoring, steering the project

⏱ When
Define, Measure, Analyze, Design, Verify

◎ Goals
- Attain the project goal with existing resources
- Stick to the timeframe and budget
- Establish suitable planning and steering elements

▶▶ Steps
Project Management can be structured as follows:

Successful Project Management is characterized by a few key features:
- An interdisciplinary team,
- Detailed project planning,
- Clear definition of areas of competence for project and line functions,
- Early integration of all involved areas as well as external partners (customers, suppliers, test institutes, universities, etc.),
- Use of effective and efficient planning and steering elements,
- Continuous project monitoring and steering,
- Structured documentation of information,
- Targeted and structured communication within the team and beyond the company.

40

Activities, Time and Resource Planning

Term / Description
Project schedule, planning activities, timeframes and resources

When
Define, Measure, Analyze, Design, Verify

Goals
- Determine the project milestones
- Identify the activities
- Assign the resources
- Visualize the interdependencies (time and content)

Steps
The structuring into phases follows the DMADV approach. The Gate Reviews taking place at the end of a phase are the main milestones of the project (see Gate Reviews).
The activities in each phase are planned in detail.

Project Plan based on DMADV *(examplary)*

	Activity	
DEFINE	Initiating the project	Draw up the Business Plan
		Define problems and goals
		Assess monetary benefit
		Define roles
	Scoping the project	Set the project scope (in / out)
		Develop the MGP
		Examine influence of other projects
	Managing the project	Complete the Project Charter
		Draw up project plan and schedule
		Set budget
		Plan resources
		Change Management
		Risk Management

41

DEFINE

MEASURE

ANALYZE

DESIGN

VERIFY

MEASURE

Activity	
Selecting customers	Identify customers
	Formulate hypotheses on customer requirements
	Formulate hypotheses on customer behavior in the process
	Plan customer studies and surveys
Collecting customer voices	Observe the customers in the process
	Interview customers
	Identify target costs
Specifying customer requirements	Derive and assess customer needs
	Derive CTQs and output measurements
	Define target values and output measurements
	Assess risks
	Review the relevance of the CTQs with the customer

ANALYZE

Activity	
Identifying the design concept	Analyze functions
	Derive the relationships between system functions and output measurements
	Develop different high-level concepts
Optimizing the design concept	Resolve conflicts in the selected high-level concept
	Identify the resources necessary for realization
Reviewing the capabilities of the concept	Collect feedback from customers and stakeholders
	Finalize high-level concept
	Assess development risks

DESIGN

Activity	
Developing, testing and optimizing the detailed concept	Elaborate the concept in detail
Reviewing performance for target production	Examine the system capacity
	Optimize system (product / process)
	Gather feedback from customers and stakeholders
	Freeze the system design
Developing and optimizing lean process	Prepare process management
	Draw up a pilot plan
	Draw up control and reaction plan
	Inform involved employees

DEFINE

Activity		
VERIFY	Preparing implementation	Set up KPI (Key Performance Indicator) system
		Set up process monitoring
		Draw up process management diagram
		Pilot the process
	Implementing the process	Draw up the final SOPs and process documentation
		Carry out implementation
	Handing over the process	Hand over process documentation
		Conclude the project
		Conduct Gate Review

The time allotted to the respective activities is determined with respect to the start and end dates.

Scheduling
Example: Measure Phase

	Activity		Duration [days]	Start	End
MEASURE	Selecting customers	Identify customers	1	7.6	7.7
		Formulate hypotheses on customer requirements	1	7.7	7.8
		Formulate hypotheses on customer behavior in the process	1	7.8	7.9
		Plan customer studies and surveys	3	7.9	7.12
	Collecting customer voices	Observe the customers in the process	3	7.12	7.15
		Interview customers	5	7.15	7.20
		Identify target costs	3	7.20	7.23
	Specifying customer requirements	Derive and assess customer needs	1	7.23	7.24
		Derive CTQs and output measurements	1	7.24	7.25
		Define target values and output measurements	1	7.25	7.26
		Assess risks	1	7.26	7.27
		Review the relevance of the CTQs with the customer	1	7.27	7.28

The time needed for each activity is recorded in a Gantt Chart; this chart visualizes the activities which run parallel.

MEASURE

ANALYZE

DESIGN

VERIFY

43

DEFINE

MEASURE

ANALYZE

DESIGN

VERIFY

Gantt Chart
Excerpt for the Measure Phase

<table>
<tr><th colspan="2">Activity</th><th colspan="4">September</th><th colspan="4">October</th><th colspan="4">November</th></tr>
<tr><th></th><th></th><th>1</th><th>2</th><th>3</th><th>4</th><th>1</th><th>2</th><th>3</th><th>4</th><th>1</th><th>2</th><th>3</th><th>4</th></tr>
<tr><td rowspan="4">Selecting customers</td><td>Identify customers</td><td>■</td><td></td><td></td><td></td><td></td><td></td><td></td><td></td><td></td><td></td><td></td><td></td></tr>
<tr><td>Formulate hypotheses on customer requirements</td><td></td><td>■</td><td></td><td></td><td></td><td></td><td></td><td></td><td></td><td></td><td></td><td></td></tr>
<tr><td>Formulate hypotheses on customer behavior in the process</td><td></td><td></td><td>■</td><td>■</td><td></td><td></td><td></td><td></td><td></td><td></td><td></td><td></td></tr>
<tr><td>Plan customer studies and surveys</td><td></td><td></td><td></td><td></td><td>■</td><td></td><td></td><td></td><td></td><td></td><td></td><td></td></tr>
<tr><td rowspan="3">Collecting customer voices</td><td>Observe the customers in the process</td><td></td><td></td><td></td><td></td><td></td><td>■</td><td></td><td></td><td></td><td></td><td></td><td></td></tr>
<tr><td>Interview customers</td><td></td><td></td><td></td><td></td><td></td><td></td><td>■</td><td></td><td></td><td></td><td></td><td></td></tr>
<tr><td>Identify target costs</td><td></td><td></td><td></td><td></td><td></td><td></td><td></td><td>■</td><td></td><td></td><td></td><td></td></tr>
<tr><td rowspan="5">Specifying customer require- ments</td><td>Derive and assess customer needs</td><td></td><td></td><td></td><td></td><td></td><td></td><td></td><td>■</td><td></td><td></td><td></td><td></td></tr>
<tr><td>Derive CTQs and output measurements</td><td></td><td></td><td></td><td></td><td></td><td></td><td></td><td></td><td>■</td><td></td><td></td><td></td></tr>
<tr><td>Define target values and output measurements</td><td></td><td></td><td></td><td></td><td></td><td></td><td></td><td></td><td></td><td>■</td><td></td><td></td></tr>
<tr><td>Assess risks</td><td></td><td></td><td></td><td></td><td></td><td></td><td></td><td></td><td></td><td></td><td>■</td><td></td></tr>
<tr><td>Review the relevance of the CTQs with the customer</td><td></td><td></td><td></td><td></td><td></td><td></td><td></td><td></td><td></td><td></td><td></td><td>■</td></tr>
</table>

⇒ Tips

- A Network Plan should be employed for more complex development projects. Based on a Gantt Chart, the Network Plan visualizes the inter-dependencies between the activities which, because of their planning in sequential and parallel execution, generate a complex network of connections. The Network Plan visualizes the critical path through the project. The critical path marks the interdependent activities which form the longest sequence. Thus the date for project conclusion can be set. See the respective project management literature for further information.
- To ensure a successful conclusion, single activities are often granted generous time reserves when planning (as a rule 50-200%).
- These time reserves are to be shortened in consultation with the persons responsible and should instead be reallocated as a buffer for the whole project to the end of the critical path. This ensures that the single activities are carried out more quickly. The buffer helps all involved persons to stick to the planned end date and is not simply "wasted".
- Deviations from the schedule should always be made visible in the charts, comparing the targeted with the actual times.
- The content and purpose of the single activities must be clearly defined during project work. Otherwise there is a risk that they are not implemented in the way the team wants!

Resources are allocated to the planned activities. The following issues should be considered:
- Are team members released from their daily routine or do they also have to deal with other tasks?
- Who is the contact partner when conflicts between project and line organization emerge?
- When are team members not available due to vacation, training programs, etc.?
- Is external support required?

The responsibilities of team members for single activities can be determined and visualized with the aid of a RACI Chart.

DEFINE

MEASURE

ANALYZE

DESIGN

VERIFY

RACI Chart

☐ Term / Description
RACI Chart, defining areas of responsibility

⊙ When
In the Define Phase, project management

◎ Goals
– Clearly define responsibility for main tasks
– Avoid inefficient internal communication

▶▶ Steps
– List project participants
– List the main tasks
– Assign the roles of the project participants to the main tasks:
  - **Responsible (R)**: individual responsible for carrying out / introducing a measure
  - **Accountable (A)**: only one "A" can be allocated for each main task
  - **Consulted (C)**: person to be consulted when carrying out a main task
  - **Informed (I)**: to be informed about decisions and interim results

⇒ Tips
• A clear definition of roles reduces communication problems. The RACI Chart should be drawn up as early as possible.
• To avoid resource shortages, the same team member should not be responsible for more than one main task at a time.

RACI Chart
Example of a DMADV project

R = Responsible
A = Accountable
C = Consulted
I = Informed

		Management Ms. G.	Marketing Ms. M.	R&D Dr. F.	Quality Management Dr. Q.	Procurement Mr. E.	Production Ms. P.	Sales Prof. Dr. V.	Customer Services Ms. K.
MEASURE	Identify the target market	A	R					C	
	Find out customer requirements	I	R	I					I
	Derive CTQs	I	R					R	C
	Benchmarking	I	R					R	C
	Detect improvement potentials	I							
	Technological benchmarking		I	A	R		C	I	
	Derive target values			A	R				
ANALYZE	Develop design concepts	I	C				R		I
	Select concept	I	C						
	Develop target criteria			A	R		R		
	Derive target values			A	R	C	R		
DESIGN	Elaborate detailed concept		I	A	R	C	R		
	Derive CTPs			A	R	C	R		
	Select applicable production processes			C					
	Plan new production processes			C	A	C	R		
	Derive SOPs			C	A		R		
	Select SOPs			C	A		R		
VERIFY	Plan the pilot	C	I	R	R	C	A		
	Carry out the pilot	C	I	R	R	C	A		
	Adapt the whole process	C	I	R	R	C	A		
	Plan the Roll Out	C		R	R	C	A		
	Hand over to the Process Owner	C		R	R				

DEFINE

MEASURE

ANALYZE

DESIGN

VERIFY

Project Budgeting

☐ Term / Description
Project Budgeting, planning and budget project costs

⊙ When
In the Define Phase, project management, after planning the project (activities, schedule, resource planning)

◎ Goals
– Identify the budget need for the project
– Secure a reliable planning and an efficient budget monitoring

▶▶ Steps
The required project budget is identified with the aid of a costs statement.

Cost Planning and Monitoring
Listing of positions

	Category	Detailing: What? For what? Who?	DFSS Phase (DMADV)	Project activity	Planned (Target)				Current				Deviation	
					Cost period	Net €	Pre-tax €	Tax €	Cost period	Net €	Pre-tax €	Tax €	Current target	Explanation
Budget operative	1. External services													
	2. Materials and tools													
	3. Travel costs													
	4. Investments (e.g. leases, SW licenses)													
Non-budget operative	5. Internal costs (as per internal cost rate*)													
	* Internal cost rate, the number of employees for a department [€/h]			Sum:										

The Project Manager monitors whether the project budget is met. The actual costs are compared to the originally budgeted costs.
Any differences must be explained.

⇨ **Tips**
- Work closely with the Sponsor when planning the budget! As a rule the Sponsor secures the availability of the project budget.
- Consult a controller when identifying the internal cost rates.
- The project budget must be considered when identifying the project benefit!

DEFINE

MEASURE

ANALYZE

DESIGN

VERIFY

Stakeholder Analysis

📁 **Term / Description**
Stakeholder Analysis

🕐 **When**
Define, Measure, Analyze, Design, Verify

◎ **Goals**
– Guarantee the necessary support for the project
– Identify resistance to the project and alleviate fears

▶▶ **Steps**
Every important person associated with the project is identified.
Reactions and attitudes towards the project are assessed.

Stakeholder Analysis

Stakeholder	Attitude to project					Measure
	--	-	O	+	++	
Mr. A			O	+		
Mr. B	O	+				
Mr. C		O		+		

-- strongly against, - moderately against, O neutral, + moderately in favor, ++ strongly in favor

Measures are to be formulated which raise the acceptance of the project among individuals / groups.

⇨ **Tips**
• Draw up the Stakeholder Analysis together with the Sponsor.
• To ensure the confidentiality of the analysis, consideration needs to be given to how the company usually deals with its internal conflicts and resistance to change.

The communication process is outlined in a communication plan.

Communication Plan

Content	Message and its communication
Purpose	Why is this message to be sent to the recipient?
Recipient	Who is to receive the message?
Responsibility	Who is responsible for the communication?
Media	Which media form is to be used?
Time	When is the communication to take place?
Status	Is the realization running according to schedule?

Formulating "elevator speech" guarantees a unified front between the team and the project when communicating externally. "Elevator speech" should be
– short and succinct,
– contain no negative experiences,
– increase project acceptance.

⇨ **Tips**
- Mutual trust with the contact partners is to be established and nurtured.
- Keep the feedback loops short (avoid giving the opportunity for "Chinese whispers") and do not allow rumors to spread!
- Select communication methods which are consistent and simple. This enhances understanding and thus acceptance of the project.
- For this reason make sure that up-to-date bulletins are published regularly!

DEFINE

MEASURE

ANALYZE

DESIGN

VERIFY

Change Management

🗀 Term / Description

Change Management, using the communication plan, communication process

🕓 When

Define, Measure, Analyze, Design, Verify

◎ Goals

– Formulate a stringent and effective communication process
– Draw up a communication plan

▶▶ Steps

Contact persons for the involved areas are identified.

Communication Partners

Topic	Department	Contact Person
Defining target market	Management / Marketing	Mr. G.
Market price / Amount covered	Marketing / Finances	Dr. F.
Evaluating customer wishes	Marketing / Production / Customer Services	Ms. A.
Competition analysis	Marketing / Development	Ms. B.
Design concepts	Development / Production	Dr. C.
Production	Production / Quality Management / Suppliers	Dr. Z.
Organization	Production / HR	Mr. H.
Sales & Distribution	Sales & Distribution	Ms. D.
After Sales Service	Customer Services	Ms. M.

The selected contact persons are to be informed and motivated.

The following questions are helpful for finding the communication form suitable for each contact partner:
- Which instruments or media are to be used for communicating?
- What is the purpose of communication?
- Who is responsible for which communication tasks?
- When, how often, and how long should communication take place?

DEFINE

MEASURE

ANALYZE

DESIGN

VERIFY

DEFINE

MEASURE

ANALYZE

DESIGN

VERIFY

Risk Assessment

📁 **Term / Description**
Risk Assessment, Risk Analysis

🕐 **When**
Define, Measure, Analyze, Design, Verify

◎ **Goal**
Assess the risks in terms of their probable occurrence and influence on project success

▶▶ **Steps**
Risks are identified and their possible impact on project success is analyzed.
The probability that these risks occur must be estimated.
This information can then be characterized by using a Risk Management Matrix.

Risk Management Matrix

Probability of occurrence	Low influence	Moderate influence	High influence
High	Moderate risk	High risk	Show stopper
Moderate	Low risk	Moderate risk	High risk
Low	Low risk	Low risk	Moderate risk

Influence on project success: Low — Moderate — High

☐ Reduce before continuing the project or stop the project
■ Minimize or control risks
☐ Proceed with caution

54

Project-specific risks are classified according to their influence. Distinctions are drawn between the following risks:

- Business risks, e.g. capital investments required in order to bring the project to a successful end
- Economic risks which could influence the project
- Political risks
- Technological risks which could have an impact on the execution of the project
- Change Management risks, i.e. risks that may emerge due to the company culture and structure

Risk Classification

Example

Risk Type	Frequently observed project risks
Business	Supplies (departments, subcontractors, customers, etc.) are delayed
Technological	The feasibility of technological implementation is questionable
Change Management	Resources are not available (personnel, computers, testing opportunities, etc.)
	Employees refuse to accept the project
	Company internal wrangling over responsibility and leadership

Evaluating risks allows measures to be introduced prior to the project's launch.

⇨ **Tip**

To enable prompt action the Sponsor should be informed about high risks as early as possible. Otherwise the progress of the project can then make the respective action impossible!

DEFINE

MEASURE

ANALYZE

DESIGN

VERIFY

DEFINE

MEASURE

ANALYZE

DESIGN

VERIFY

Kick-off Meeting

📁 **Term / Description**
Kick-off Meeting

🕐 **When**
At the beginning of the Define Phase, the first meeting of the whole project team

◎ **Goals**
- Integrate team members into the project
- Explain the importance of the project for the company
- Inform the team members on their roles so that they can perform these to their full capacity
- Attain the Sponsor's agreement on the project

▸▸ **Steps**
- Agree with the Sponsor on the date and ensure his / her attendance
- Discuss the key points of the Project Charter with potential team members personally. The involvement of the Sponsor can be helpful.
- Develop the agenda in consultation with the Sponsor and Master Black Belt. Hold the meeting in line with this agenda.
- Invite team members, including those on the periphery. The official invitation to the Kick-off Meeting should contain the following:
  - Title,
  - Agenda (schedule),
  - Objectives,
  - List of participants.
- Organize suitable venue. Make sure that there are sufficient materials for moderating the meeting (e.g. markers, metaplan charts, flip charts, paper).
- The function and suitability of the technical aids should be checked beforehand.
- Draw up a protocol / documentation.

Gate Review

📁 **Term/Description**
Gate Review, phase check, phase assessment

🕐 **When**
At the conclusion of each phase: Define, Measure, Analyze, Design, Verify

◎ **Goals**
- Inform the Sponsor about the results and measures of the respective phase
- Assess the results
- Decide on the further course of the project

▶▶ **Steps**
The results are presented in full and in an easily comprehensible form.

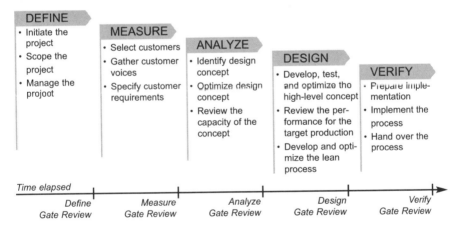

The Sponsor is to examine the status of the project on the basis of the following criteria:
- Results are complete,
- Probability of project success,
- Resources are optimally allocated in the project.

57

DEFINE

MEASURE

ANALYZE

DESIGN

VERIFY

The Sponsor decides if the project can enter the next phase.

All of the results from the Define Phase are presented to the Sponsor and Stakeholders in the Gate Review. The following questions must be answered in a complete and comprehensible presentation:

On initiating the project:
- Which problem is the occasion for the project?
- What is the goal of the project?
- Who are the target customers?
- What are the prospective benefits of the project and how have these been identified?
- What is the current market and competition situation?

On scoping the project:
- Which aspects form the content of the project?
- Which do not?
- What is the influence on other projects?
- Which development is being striven for in the long term? What is the vision?

On managing the project:
- Who are the team members and why have they been selected?
- How were the roles and responsibilities in the core team defined?
- Which activities and resources were required?
- What kind of timeframe and budget are needed?
- On what basis was this data identified?
- What is the project's level of acceptance?
- What are the risks?
- Which measures have been / are to be introduced as a result?

Design for Six Sigma^{+Lean} Toolset

MEASURE

DEFINE

MEASURE

ANALYZE

DESIGN

VERIFY

Phase 2: Measure

Goals

- Identify customers and their needs
- Derive the specific requirements to the system (product / process)
- Determine the corresponding output measurements and their target values and tolerances

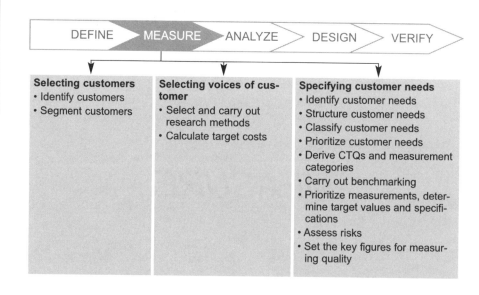

| DEFINE | MEASURE | ANALYZE | DESIGN | VERIFY |

Selecting customers
- Identify customers
- Segment customers

Selecting voices of customer
- Select and carry out research methods
- Calculate target costs

Specifying customer needs
- Identify customer needs
- Structure customer needs
- Classify customer needs
- Prioritize customer needs
- Derive CTQs and measurement categories
- Carry out benchmarking
- Prioritize measurements, determine target values and specifications
- Assess risks
- Set the key figures for measuring quality

Steps

A roadmap for the Measure Phase is presented on the opposite page.

Most Important Tools

- ABC Classification
- Portfolio Analysis
- 5W1H Table
- Survey Techniques
- Customer Interaction Study
- Affinity Chart
- Tree Diagram

- Kano Model
- Analytic Hierarchy Process
- House of Quality
- Benchmarking
- Design Scorecard

Measure Roadmap

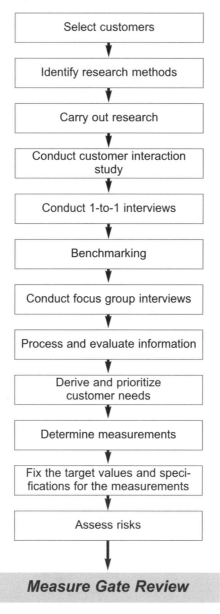

DEFINE

MEASURE

ANALYZE

DESIGN

VERIFY

Select customers

↓

Identify research methods

↓

Carry out research

↓

Conduct customer interaction study

↓

Conduct 1-to-1 interviews

↓

Benchmarking

↓

Conduct focus group interviews

↓

Process and evaluate information

↓

Derive and prioritize customer needs

↓

Determine measurements

↓

Fix the target values and specifications for the measurements

↓

Assess risks

↓

Measure Gate Review

Sponsor: Go / No-go Decision

Selecting Customers

☐ **Term/Description**
Customer selection

🕑 **When**
Prior to project launch in the Define and Measure Phases

◎ **Goal**
Focus on the customers who are most important for the project's success

▶▶ **Steps**

Customer Interaction with Systems

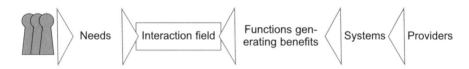

Needs · Interaction field · Functions generating benefits · Systems · Providers

Identifying Customers

☐ Term / Description
Customer Identification, part of Customer Selection process

◔ When
Prior to project launch, in the Define & Measure Phases

◎ Goal
Identify the target market and the target customers

▶▶ Steps
The whole market is segmented and a segment selected as the target market. Relevant target customers in this segment are then identified using suitable methods.

Market Segmentation

Examples of the target customers of the system which is to be developed are:
- Final consumer / user
- Purchase deciders
- Purchase influencers

The target customers are characterized and segmented with the aid of specified criteria.

Segmentation Criteria for Customers

Customers in consumer markets	Customers in markets of commercial customers and organizations
• Demographic: age, sex, size of location, city/rural, region • Sociographic: profession, income, education, household size, marital status, religion • Psychographic: personality type, lifestyle, life stages, life goals	• Type of company, authority, organization • Branches, economic sector, business model • Size of business • Non-customer, potential buyer, customer • Region, location, situation • Position within the value chain • Assets, utilization • Buying behavior

⇢ **Tips**

- Ideas on the target customers/target market should be formulated before the launch of the DFSS project. This includes the proportion between new customers and existing customers. These aspects are to be documented in a provisional Business Case that will be validated over the course of the Measure Phase.
- The marketing or sales departments should be able to provide all necessary information.
- The DFSS team is not to carry out the corresponding market and competition analysis!
- The target customers identified are to be prioritized. Customers contributing financially to the value chain are to be given the highest priority, along with the final consumers/users.

ABC Classification

📁 Term/Description
ABC Classification

🕑 When
Prior to project launch, in the Define & Measure Phases

◎ Goal
Focus on the target customers who generate the largest turnover share

▶▶ Steps
Existing customers are assessed by considering their respective share in company turnover. Turnover from the past year or forecasted turnover serves as the basis.
If turnover fluctuates strongly, then the average turnover over the past 3 years is calculated and taken as the basis. Contribution margins can also be applied as a comparison.

ABC Classification

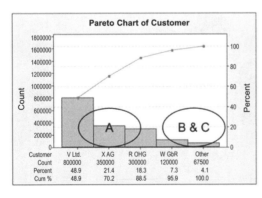

Existing customers are divided into:
A-customers with 80% turnover share,
B-customers with up to 15% turnover share and
C-customers with only 5% turnover share.

DEFINE

MEASURE

ANALYZE

DESIGN

VERIFY

Portfolio Analysis

📁 **Term / Description**
Portfolio Analysis

🕘 **When**
Prior to the project launch, in the Define & Measure Phases

◎ **Goal**
Supplement the ABC classification with relevant information on potential market growth

▶▶ **Step**
A third dimension (e.g. the market growth of the trade channel) is added to the two-dimensional ABC classification.

Portfolio Analysis

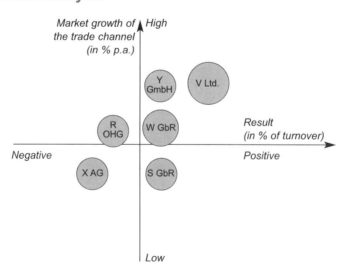

The size of the circle depicted represents the turnover in a third dimension.

5W1H Table

📁 **Term/Description**
5W1H Table

🕐 **When**
In the Measure Phase, selecting customers

◎ **Goal**
Derive and structure existing information and formulate hypotheses on the interaction between selected target customers and the system (product/process)

▶▶ **Step**
Structure the existing information and hypotheses on the basis of the five W's and one H: Who? What? When? Where? Why? How?

Target Customer Table
Example: passenger seat

Who	What	When	Where	Wy	How
Commuters – 80% share	Use the bus to commute to work; take up to 50% of seats	Between 6-10 a.m. and 3-7 p.m.	Use the seats primarily in the area of entrance-exit doors	Quicker entrance and exit from bus. Seats usually not too dirty	Cleaner and comfortable seats with sufficient legroom
Schoolchildren – 15% share	Use the bus to travel to school; take up to 60% of seats	Between 8-10 a.m. and 12-2 p.m.	Use the seats primarily in rear area of bus	Seats arranged in benches, allowing groups	Enough room to sit in groups
Students – 5% share	Use the bus to travel to university – take up to 20% of seats	Between 8-10 a.m. and 2-6 p.m.	Use the seats primarily in front of bus, behind the driver cabin	Quicker entrance and exit, no need to move through the bus	Cleaner and comfortable seats with sufficient legroom
Bus operator	Operates the bus line service	Monday to Sunday, 6 a.m. - 10 p.m.	Moscow + 50 km around		

Collecting Customer Voices

☐ Term / Description
Voice of the customer (VOC)

🕐 When
In the Measure Phase, collecting customer voices

◎ Goal
Identify and collect the relevant information on the target customers and their needs

▶▶ Steps
Internal and external research of information on target customers

DEFINE

MEASURE

ANALYZE

DESIGN

VERIFY

Selecting and Carrying out Research Methods

📁 **Term/Description**
Research

🕐 **When**
In the Measure Phase, selecting customer voices

◎ **Goal**
- Select the methods suitable for gathering all the information relevant for deriving target customer needs
- Avoid imprecision when identifying needs – this reduces the risk of mis-guided development
- Significantly reduce the process lead time of a development project by systematically preparing data collection

▶▶ **Steps**
Select and apply the methods most suitable for gathering relevant information

Research methods are presented on the following page.

DEFINE

MEASURE

ANALYZE

DESIGN

VERIFY

Research Method Table

INTERNAL	*Passive*	*Internal research*	Research in secondary sources on customer needs and require-ments, customer values, possible product and service qualities, indicators for measuring success.
EXTERNAL	*Active*	*Customer interaction study*	Observe the customer "at work" to gain a better understanding of his environment and activities. Identify needs. This delivers information on unexpressed needs in particular.
		1-to-1 interview	Provides results on the needs and expectations of specific cus-tomers, their values, their views of service aspects, desired product / service attributes, and data for measuring success.
		Focus group interview	The focus group is suitable for identifying the general view of a group of customers. The group should represent a specific cus-tomer segment and in this way supports the precise definition of the segment as well as prioritizing customer values.
		Survey	Serves to measure customer needs and values as well as evalu-ate products and services on the basis of a large number of cus-tomers from one or several segments. When based on a large sample this provides "hard" facts for decision-making.

⇨ **Tip**

Make sure that internal and external methods for observing and surveying customers are combined sensibly; this means that the pros and cons of the individual methods are taken into account, enabling a comprehensive research picture.

70

Internal Research

☐ **Term/Description**
Internal research, passive research

🕐 **When**
In the Measure Phase, collecting customer voices

◎ **Goals**
- Collect and structure sensibly all existing information on the target customers
- Generate the first hypotheses on possible customer needs
- Identify information gaps
- Prepare external customer surveys

▶▶ **Steps**
The following secondary sources contain relevant information and can provide indicators of possible customer needs:
- Information from service or sales departments,
- Customer complaints,
- Specialist journals,
- Internet,
- Patents, etc.

⇢ **Tip**
Internal research, when used as a cost-effective method, should be seen purely as a preparation for more in-depth external research.
Internal research will never be able to provide all of the information necessary to gain a complete profile of customer needs. Its main purpose is to help formulate hypotheses about customer behavior and needs, which are then verified or discarded through external research methods.

DEFINE

MEASURE

ANALYZE

DESIGN

VERIFY

External Research

☐ Term / Descriptio
External research, active research

🕐 When
In the Measure Phase, collecting customer voices

◎ Goals
- Actively collect the relevant information on target customers
- Verify the hypotheses on possible customer needs formulated in the internal research

▶▶ Step
Generate information directly with the customers.
Observe the customer(s) on site in interaction with the system.

DEFINE

Customer Interaction Study

⬜ Term/Description
Customer Interaction Study, Customer Relationship Modeling, Going to the Gemba, Gemba Study

🕑 When
In the Measure Phase, collecting customer voices

MEASURE

◎ Goals
– Gain undistorted and complete information on the customer(s)
– Identify the actual customer needs (without considering solutions at this stage)

▶▶ Steps
The Customer Interaction Study involves three steps:
1. Planning,
2. Execution,
3. Analysis.

ANALYZE

1. Planning
Determine the study's who, what, when, where, and how. The team formulates hypotheses on the customer's interaction with the system (product/process). It is very helpful to visualize the interaction process when formulating the hypotheses.
A Customer Interaction Study is not limited to simply asking questions; the customer's environment and the customers are observed with great attention to detail. A Customer Interaction Study is carried out where value originates for the customer(s).

DESIGN

Customer values are presented on the following page.

VERIFY

DEFINE

MEASURE

ANALYZE

DESIGN

VERIFY

Example of Customer Values

Customer values

1. Solves an existing problem
2. Helps open up new opportunities
3. Helps the customer to look good vis-à-vis competitors
4. Helps the customer to feel good

Reliability

2. Execution

The environment, situation, and behavior of the customers are documented. The voice of the customer is noted.

Needs identified during the Interaction Study are to be confirmed by the observed customer whenever possible.

A standard form should be used by all "observers" for documenting the information.

Form for Customer Interaction Study
Example: passenger seat

1 Planning		
Observer name:	Peter Finger	
Date and time:	October 23, 2005 - 12.30 p.m.	
Location:	Moscow, busing parking lot of AutoMoskov	
Name of observed person:	Sergej Abramovic	
Contact details:	Sergej.abramovic@hotmail.com	
Details on observed person:	Sergej Abramovic works for AutoMoskov as fitter and is primarily responsible for bus interiors	
Current environment/ situation:	Sergej Abramovic is stressed because of an accident in Moscow's inner city this morning. He has to return to local authorities to make a statement.	

2 Execution						3 Analysis		
Process step	Observation	Verbatim statement	Medium	Notes			Recognized need	Verified by observed person? (yes/no)
#4: uninstall old seat	Has to loosen 8 bolts with a wrench	"Shit, this is taking too long."	Notepad	He wants to finish the installation work before he returns to the city.			Quick assembly and installation of seats	Yes
		"The bolts are rusted again."					Simple assembly and installation of seats	Yes
		"The bolts are extremely dirty and I can't get a good grip with this wrench."						

74

3. Analysis

The hypotheses formulated in the planning are now discarded, adjusted, or verified.

The following questions form the focus of the analysis:
– What do the customers really want?
– What are their "real" needs?
– What is of value (benefit) for the customer(s)?

⇨ **Tips**

- The observer team should be interdisciplinary in its composition in order to generate as many different perspectives as possible.
- Deploying teams working parallel is a sensible move.
- Observations should be documented in detail, using video, audio, photos, drawings, and notes; here the rule is: the more information the better!
- A typical Customer Interaction Study lasts around two hours.
- Customers often give voice to possible solutions. The goal is however, to identify the real needs, i.e. the needs which form the basis of these possible solutions! A table of customer needs helps to differentiate between solutions, specifications, complaints, etc. and real needs.

DEFINE

MEASURE

ANALYZE

DESIGN

VERIFY

1-to-1 Interview

Term/Description
1-to-1 Interview

When
In the Measure Phase, collecting customer voices

Goal
Survey customers individually to gather further information and find out their needs and wishes

Steps
An interview guideline must be drawn up before talking to the customer. It is important to formulate open questions, i.e. questions which demand a more detailed and informative answer than just "yes" or "no".

An interview should follow a set structure:
- Explain the reason for the interview
- Explain the interview style
- Ask for permission to record the interview (audio)
- Ask the open questions in line with the prepared guideline
- Review the insights generated and, if necessary, the ideas developed together with the customer in additional questions and comments

1-to-1 Interviews: Advantages and Disadvantages

Advantages of interviews	Disadvantages of interviews
• Flexibility when dealing individually with an interview partner • Possible to cover more complex issues • High response rates	• Cost intensive • Time intensive • Requires that the interviewer is a "good listener" • Runs the risk that the interviewer and partner fail to understand one another • Different results can be generated by different interviewers

Focus Group Interview

☐ Term / Description
Focus Group Interview

◷ When
In the Measure Phase, collecting customer voices

◎ Goal
Identify the needs of a clearly defined customer group

▸▸ Steps
A Focus Group Interview is conducted during a discussion meeting where the goals, agenda, and schedule are arranged beforehand. A focus group of between 7 and 13 participants is formed by persons from the relevant customer segment. A moderator is nominated and it is his task to ensure that the focus on the theme is not lost during the discussion. This type of interview should take no longer than 2-4 hours.

Focus Group Interview: Advantages and Disadvantages

Advantages of focus group interviews	Disadvantages of focus group interviews
• Participants encourage and inspire one another: one participant says something another hadn't thought of • More cost-effective than many 1-to-1 interviews	• They are difficult to manage when the persons in the group have conflicts with each other • People tend to follow others, or become passive. This can lead to a situation where only the needs of the "dominant" person are articulated • The time available belongs to the group as a whole; not every person receives the same "airtime"

DEFINE

MEASURE

ANALYZE

DESIGN

VERIFY

DEFINE

MEASURE

ANALYZE

DESIGN

VERIFY

Survey

📁 **Term / Description**
Survey

🕐 **When**
In the Measure Phase, collecting customer voices

◎ **Goal**
Gain representative information on target customers, above all in consumer goods markets

▸▸ **Steps**
Determine and prepare the strategy, then carry out and analyze the survey. A structured questionnaire is to be developed that shall aid in surveying the customers. A statistically representative type and number of customers is to be surveyed. Samples are therefore required beforehand.
Depending on the customer segment and the project scope, various kinds of surveys can be used and combined with another.

Examples of Survey Types

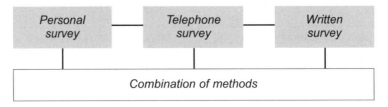

Personal survey	Telephone survey	Written survey
Combination of methods		

Personal surveys
make sense when complex issues need to be clarified. The information required can be generated in full.
– Personal surveys are generally more expensive than telephone or written surveys.

DEFINE

- The training effort for interviewers is high, because experience as well as a high level of social, and often technological, competence is required.

Telephone surveys
make sense when a large number of target customers is to be surveyed within a short period of time.
- They generate a result quickly.
- The interviewer's influence on the results is low.
- Limiting the scope of the survey to only those customers reachable by telephone distorts the results.
- More complex issues cannot be adequately answered.

MEASURE

Written surveys
make sense when the budget and resources shall be disburdened.
- Far fewer personnel is required to send a questionnaire per e-mail or post.
- The cost of sending e-mails or using postal services is irrespective of the size of the questionnaire.
- Households with internet connection may not be representative of the selected customer segment.
- Return rates and the information gained are generally lower than that of the other methods.

ANALYZE

Questionnaires for surveys
Special care is needed when compiling the questionnaire.
- All hypotheses formulated during internal research or the customer Interaction Study are to be covered.
- The structure is to be logical and clear.
- Complex issues have to be formulated in a comprehensive way; in some cases a picture says more than a thousand words!
- A professional layout and appearance is a must.
- A personal note should inform the recipient about the reason for the survey, guarantee that all information will be treated confidentially, and should list contact persons in case there are any questions.
- Filling out the questionnaire should not take longer than 30 minutes.

DESIGN

Advantages and disadvantages are presented on the following page.

VERIFY

Surveys: Advantages and Disadvantages

Advantages of questionnaire surveys	Disadvantages of questionnaire surveys
• A significant number of market players can be surveyed • Statistically valid statements are thus possible • Evaluations and results emerging from up-to-date questionnaires are often mirrored by the strong interest shown by the respondents	• Answers are limited to the questions asked – for this reason the themes are to be worked out beforehand with other survey and observation methods • Demands a great deal of effort and expense, coupled with low return rates or refusal to participate • Negative attitude amongst the population towards questionnaire surveys

Selecting the respondents
Three methods are used for gaining a representative selection of respondents.

Selection Methods

Random Selection	Quota Selection	Haphazard Selection
For an unqualified random selection, each unit must have the same calculable chance. This method is applied for example in "random digit dialing" for telephone interviews, where the number is generated randomly and dialed automatically.	Here rules are set for selecting the respondents. They are to be designed to gain as representative a selection as possible. However: only the quota attributes are sure to be representative.	Haphazard selection means selecting occurs without any recognizable strategy. This can lead to a systematic distortion. This practice can be applied in probes or when the budget is limited and no other approach is possible. In general though, it is to be avoided.

Number of respondents
When conducting a customer survey it would be ideal to have a complete sample. But in reality a complete survey is usually not possible due to time and financial restrictions. In this case a survey that includes a representative sample size should be carried out.

⇨ Tips

- A Customer Interaction Study is an absolute must for every development project. Such a study reveals the potential for genuine breakthrough innovations!
- Against all odds, a way should always be found to carry out such a study on site.
- 1-to-1 and focus group interviews are especially suitable for target customer surveys in the sector of industrial goods markets.
- Surveys are particularly suitable for target customers in consumer goods markets.
- The survey should be planned, carried out, and analyzed together with experts from market research.
- Nothing replaces direct contact and interaction with the target customers. The biggest mistake is to assume that one already knows everything about the customer(s) and to identify their needs solely from a meeting.
- Systems (products/processes) developed on the basis of incomplete and unverified hypotheses will most likely demand a great deal of rework and fail to highlight possible breakthrough innovation.

DEFINE

MEASURE

ANALYZE

DESIGN

VERIFY

DEFINE

MEASURE

ANALYZE

DESIGN

VERIFY

Target Costing

🗀 Term / Description
Target Costing

⏲ When
In the Measure Phase, collecting customer voices

◎ Goals
– Identify a market price acceptable for the customer(s)
– Set the financial framework for margins, customer needs, and costs

▸▸ Steps
Target costs represent the "allowable" costs of a system (product / process) over its lifecycle – from the idea to its realization. Target costs are determined on the basis of the price accepted by the customer(s) and the envisioned margin.

Target costs = target price - target margin

The target price is essentially dependent on three factors:
– Customers,
– Competitor offers, and
– Strategic goals.

Target Costing

82

DEFINE

The target costs are calculated by the difference between target price and target margin. In the further course of the project these can be broken down and distributed to all the cost drivers in the system.

Target Costing

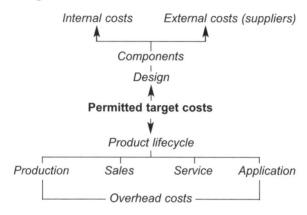

MEASURE

⇨ **Tips**
- If the design of the system (product / process) provides the customer with a significant added value vis-à-vis competing systems, he is usually willing to accept a higher price (value based pricing).
- Added value is generated through:
  - Savings in costs and time (e.g. elimination of maintenance costs)
  - Innovation (e.g. new functions not or only insufficiently covered by competing systems)
- The development team should view the target costs as a limit that may only then be exceeded when a higher price can be achieved through added value.
- The distribution of the target costs to the cost drivers becomes more detailed as the project progresses.

ANALYZE

DESIGN

VERIFY

DEFINE

MEASURE

ANALYZE

DESIGN

VERIFY

Specifying Customer Needs

☐ Term / Description
Customer Need Specification

🕐 When
Measure

◎ Goals
- Structure and prioritize real customer needs
- Determine the corresponding measurements with target values and tolerances

▶▶ Steps
- Identify, structure, classify, and prioritize customer needs
- Translate these into corresponding measurements with target values and tolerances

84

Identifying Customer Needs

📁 **Term/Description**
Customer Need Identification

🕒 **When**
In the Measure Phase, specifying customer needs

◎ **Goal**
Identify real customer needs

▸▸ **Steps**
Identify real customer needs from the information gathered about the customer

"Real" Customer Needs

DEFINE

MEASURE

ANALYZE

DESIGN

VERIFY

DEFINE

MEASURE

ANALYZE

DESIGN

VERIFY

Customer Needs Table

🗀 **Term / Description**
Customer Needs Table

🕒 **When**
In the Measure Phase, specifying customer needs

◎ **Goal**
Identify real customer needs

▶▶ **Steps**
- Assign the information gathered while collecting VOCs to the categories of the Customer Needs Table, i.e. needs, solutions, complaints, etc.
- Identify the real needs from the information.
- Formulate customer needs positively: "I would like…" instead of "I don't want" or "It should be…".

⇨ **Tip**
Abstracting the information into solution-neutral formulations of needs is critical to success!
The step supports the team to overcome psychological barriers and design genuine breakthrough innovations.

86

Customer Needs Table

Example: passenger seat

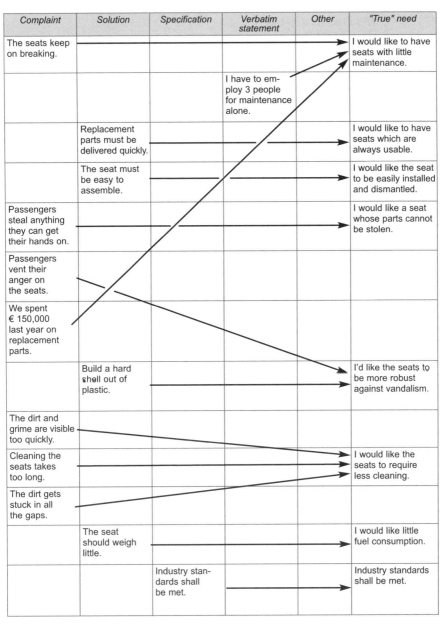

Complaint	Solution	Specification	Verbatim statement	Other	"True" need
The seats keep on breaking.					I would like to have seats with little maintenance.
			I have to employ 3 people for maintenance alone.		
	Replacement parts must be delivered quickly.				I would like to have seats which are always usable.
	The seat must be easy to assemble.				I would like the seat to be easily installed and dismantled.
Passengers steal anything they can get their hands on.					I would like a seat whose parts cannot be stolen.
Passengers vent their anger on the seats.					
We spent € 150,000 last year on replacement parts.					
	Build a hard shell out of plastic.				I'd like the seats to be more robust against vandalism.
The dirt and grime are visible too quickly.					
Cleaning the seats takes too long.					I would like the seats to require less cleaning.
The dirt gets stuck in all the gaps.					
	The seat should weigh little.				I would like little fuel consumption.
		Industry standards shall be met.			Industry standards shall be met.

87

Structuring Customer Needs

☐ Term / Description
Customer Needs Structure

◔ When
In the Measure Phase, specifying customer needs

◎ Goal
Sort customer needs

▶▶ Steps
- Arrange the identified customer needs into clusters based on their concrete content.
- Depict the hierarchy of needs.

Affinity Diagram

Term/Description
Affinity Diagram

When
In the Measure Phase, specifying customer needs

Goals
- Sort the identified customer needs into clusters based on their affinity
- Gain an understanding of how customers think

Steps
Note down customer needs on index cards or Post-It stickers and arrange them into groups according to the "main needs".

Affinity Diagram
Example: passenger seat

Maintenance
- I would like to have seats with little maintenance
- I would like to have seats which are always usable
- I would like the seat to be easily installed and dismantled
- I would like a seat whose parts cannot be stolen
- I'd like the seats to be more robust against vandalism

Cleaning
- I would like the seats to require less cleaning

Fuel consumption
- I would like less fuel consumption

Adherence to laws and standards
- I'd like to meet industry standards
- I'd like to keep laws and regulations

DEFINE

MEASURE

ANALYZE

DESIGN

VERIFY

Tree Diagram

🗀 **Term/Description**

Tree Diagram

🕐 **When**

In the Measure Phase, specifying customer needs

◎ **Goals**

- Sort the identified customer needs into clusters on the basis of their concrete content
- Identify existing needs gaps
- Create unified levels of detail
- Gain an understanding of how customers think

▶▶ **Steps**

Based on the structure of the Affinity Diagram, needs are entered into a Tree Diagram.

The Tree Diagram branches out into different sublevels, identifying existing gaps or needs yet to be articulated.

Translating the Affinity Diagram into a Tree Diagram

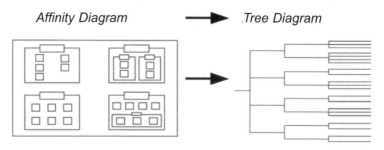

Affinity Diagram ⟶ *Tree Diagram*

DEFINE

Tree Diagram
Example: passenger seat

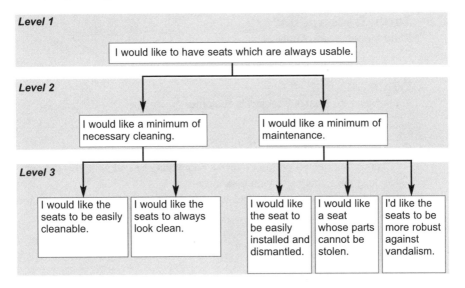

Level 1

I would like to have seats which are always usable.

Level 2

I would like a minimum of necessary cleaning.

I would like a minimum of maintenance.

Level 3

| I would like the seats to be easily cleanable. | I would like the seats to always look clean. | I would like the seat to be easily installed and dismantled. | I would like a seat whose parts cannot be stolen. | I'd like the seats to be more robust against vandalism. |

MEASURE

⇨ **Tips**

- There is no right or wrong when drawing up an Affinity Diagram. Every person thinks in different structures. If there is no direct contact with the customer, the team should undertake the preliminary work and devolop the Affinity and Tree Diagrams, which the customer is to then counter-check.
- If different needs reflecting various clusters and thinking structures emerge from the Affinity Diagrams, the team should logically structure the results.
- Tree Diagrams generate a common degree of detail and aid in identify-ing and closing thematic gaps. As the project evolves this leads to a significant reduction of misvaluations in the QFD1 (House of Quality).

ANALYZE

DESIGN

VERIFY

DEFINE

MEASURE

ANALYZE

DESIGN

VERIFY

Kano Model

📁 **Term / Description**
Kano Model*, Kano Analysis

🕐 **When**
In the Measure Phase, specifying customer needs

◎ **Goals**
- Classify expressed and not expressed customer needs into the factors of delighters, satisfiers, and dissatisfiers
- Identify and classify needs into those which the system must provide for and those it can provide for

▶▶ **Steps**
- Every potential need is reviewed with a negative and positive question for the customer:
  - How would you feel if need x is not met?
  - How would you feel if need x is met?
- The customer is given the following possible answers:
  - I'd like that
  - That's normal
  - I don't really care
  - I wouldn't like that
- Based on these customer judgments the needs can be classified into:
  - Basis factors (dissatisfiers), i.e. attributes of the system which the customer expects
  - Performance factors (satisfiers), i.e. attributes of the system by which the customer measures the system quality
  - Buzz factors (delighters), i.e. attributes of the system which exceed the customer's expectations

The following matrix helps to assign the needs to these categories.

* This classification is based on a model developed in 1978 by Prof. Dr. Noriaki Kano (University of Rika, Tokyo).

DEFINE

MEASURE

ANALYZE

DESIGN

VERIFY

Kano Table

		Answer to a negatively formulated question			
		I'd like that	Normal	I don't really care	I wouldn't like that
Answer to a positively formulated question	I'd like that		Delighter	Delighter	Satisfier
	Normal				Dissatisfier
	I don't really care				Dissatisfier
	I wouldn't like that				

Kano Model

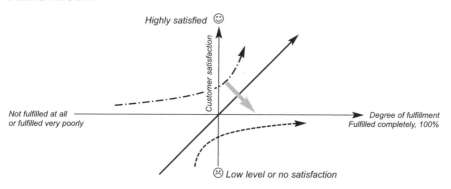

Highly satisfied ☺

Customer satisfaction

Not fulfilled at all
or fulfilled very poorly

Degree of fulfillment
Fulfilled completely, 100%

☹ Low level or no satisfaction

World-class in the market	**Assert in the market**	**Enter the market**
Delighters/buzz factors	*Satisfiers/ performance factors*	*Dissatisfiers/basis factors*
• Not expected	• Specified	• Go without saying
• Not expressed	• Expressed	• Unexpressed
• Not yet aware of	• Aware of	• Almost unaware of

⇨ **Tips**

- Categorization based on Kano is essential in order not to:
  - Furnish the system with superfluous attributes which the customers are not willing to pay for,
  - Develop a system without all the necessary attributes,
  - Develop a system based on false priorities.
- A correlation to the blank cells of the Kano table indicates a contradictory answer combination.

Prioritizing Customer Needs

☐ Term / Description

Customer Needs Prioritization

🕐 When

In the Measure Phase, specifying and prioritizing customer needs

◎ Goal

Customers prioritize the delighters and satisfiers identified in the Kano analysis

▶▶ Steps

Presented with the delighters and satisfiers identified with the aid of the Kano analysis, the customers are to weigh these factors.

Dissatisfiers are not evaluated because as basis factors or requirements they always have the highest priority. The system to be developed must be able to fulfill these to 100% at all times.

Analytic Hierarchy Process

📁 Term / Description
Analytic Hierachy Process*, AHP, pairwise comparison

🕓 When
In the Measure Phase, specifying customer needs

◎ Goal
Weigh the delighters and satisfiers in relation to one another

▶▶ Steps
The needs identified as delighters and satisfiers are structured in pairs to allow a comparative evaluation. The relative weighing of each need is calculated from weighing all paired combinations.

A scale from 1 to 9 is used for the evaluation:
1 = equally important
3 = a little more important
5 = more important
7 = much more important
9 = of extremely greater importance

A "less important" weighing in relation with "extremely greater importance" is evaluated as:
1/7 = far less weighing
1/9 = extremely less weighing

An AHP contingency table is presented on the following page.

* *Thomas L. Saaty (2000): Fundamentals of decision making and priority theory with the Analytic Hierarchy Process, vol. VI of the AHP series, RWS Publications, Pittsburg / USA*

AHP Contingency Table

Example: passenger seat

Needs	I'd like the seats to be more robust against vandalism.	I would like a seat whose parts cannot be stolen.	I would like the seat to be easily installed and dismantled.	I would like the seats to always look clean.	I would like the seats to be easily clean-able.	Aggregate relative	Relative weighing [%]
I'd like the seats to be more robust against vandalism.	1.00 / 0.38	1.00 / 0.41	5.00 / 0.35	5.00 / 0.31	0.20 / 0.01	1.46	**29.2**
I would like a seat whose parts cannot be stolen.	1.00 / 0.38	1.00 / 0.41	6.00 / 0.42	7.00 / 0.43	7.00 / 0.43	2.07	**41.3**
I would like the seat to be easily installed and dismantled.	0.20 / 0.08	0.17 / 0.07	1.00 / 0.07	3.00 / 0.18	8.00 / 0.49	0.89	**17.7**
I would like the seats to always look clean.	0.20 / 0.08	0.14 / 0.06	0.33 / 0.02	1.00 / 0.06	0.20 / 0.01	0.23	**4.6**
I would like the seats to be easily cleanable.	0.20 / 0.08	0.14 / 0.06	2.00 / 0.14	0.33 / 0.02	1.00 / 0.06	0.36	**7.1**
Aggregate	2.60	2.45	14.33	16.33	16.33		
Aggregate relative	1.00	1.00	1.00	1.00	1.00	5.00	100.00

The pair comparison proceeds from the row to the column, e.g.:
- "I'd like the seats to be more robust against vandalism" is more impor-tant (5) than "I would like the seat to be easily installed and dismantled," or:
- "I would like the seats to always look clean," is somewhat less important (1/3) than "I would like the seat to be easily installed and dismantled."

Then the aggregates of the columns are formed, e.g.:
- Column "I'd like the seats to be more robust against vandalism": 1+1+1/5+1/5+1/5 = 2.6,
- Column "I would like the seats to always look clean": 5+7+3+1+1/3 = 16.33.

The weighing of each cell is now observed and scaled in relation to the respective column aggregate, e.g.:
"I'd like the seats to be more robust against vandalism"/"I would like the seats to always look clean" in relation to the column aggregate for "I'd like the seats to be more robust against vandalis": 0.2/2.6 = 0.08.

The total weighing of the single rows is achieved by adding together their scaled cell values, e.g. the row "I'd like the seats to be more robust against vandalism":
$0.38+0.41+0.35+0.31+0.01 = 1.46$.

The column aggregate of these values corresponds to the total weighing of all rows:
$1.46+2.07+0.89+0.23+0.36 = 5.00$.

Scaling the row aggregates with this total generates the weighing of the individual needs in relation to the other needs.

⇨ **Tips**

- The pair comparison through AHP is carried out ideally by the customers or together with the customers.
- A member of the project team should be responsible for moderating the task.
- If the evaluations given by the various customers are not consistent, the mean of the different comparisons is calculated and entered into the corresponding cell of the contingency table.
- It is not recommended to generate an absolute weighing of needs using an ordinal scale (e.g. 1 = unimportant to 5 = very important) because it rarely leads to a meaningful prioritization! Experience shows that here all needs are evaluated as important or very important. This makes it impossible to identify the relative weighing or ensure the targeted deployment of available resources.

DEFINE

MEASURE

ANALYZE

DESIGN

VERIFY

Deriving CTQs and
Key Output Measurements

📁 **Term / Description**
CTQs and Key Output Measurements

🕓 **When**
In the Measure Phase, specifying customer needs

◎ **Goal**
Transform customer needs into specific and measurable customer requirements (Critical to Quality = CTQ) with the appropriate measurement categories

▶▶ **Steps**
Stick to the following rules when deriving CTQs from the identified cus-
tomer needs:
  – Describe customer requirements and not solutions
  – Describe requirements in full sentences
  – Formulate requirements which refer to a single object
  – Formulate as specifically as possible
  – Use succinct formulations
  – Formulate positively
  – Utilize measurable terms
     (Test: can the requirement be measured?)

In the next step the CTQs are assigned to the corresponding measurements. The decisive factor with respect to this is if the respective measurement can give clear hints at meeting the specific requirements.

Transformation Table
Example: passenger seat

Need	CTQ	Measurement
I'd like the seats to be more robust against vandalism.	Each seat and its parts are resistant against improper treatment.	Number of replaced elements
		Number of burn marks/ stains, etc. per seat
		Number of slashes per seat
		Number of graffiti per seat after cleaning
I would like a seat whose parts cannot be stolen.	Each seat and its parts are secure against theft.	Number of missing elements
I would like the seat to be easily installed and dismantled.	Each seat and its parts can be quickly assembled and dismantled.	Time needed for each single part
		Time needed for the whole seat
I would like the seats to always look clean.	Each seat and its parts look clean at all times.	Number of complaints due to dirt and grime
I would like the seats to be easily cleanable.	Each seat and its parts can be cleaned quickly.	Time needed for cleaning

specific **+** *measurable*

⇨ **Tips**

- It is recommended to draw up three transformation tables:
  - A table for delighters and satisfiers
  - A table for dissatisfiers (100% – "must be")
  - A table for conformity with laws, regulations, etc. (basis need: "I'd like the system to conform to laws on an international basis")
- The suitability of the assigned measurements will be reviewed and worked out in the course of the Measure Phase.

DEFINE

MEASURE

ANALYZE

DESIGN

VERIFY

Benchmarking

📁 **Term / Description**

Benchmarking, system, product and process comparison

🕐 **When**

In the Measure Phase, specifying customer needs

◎ **Goal**

Evaluate the competing systems in terms of fulfilling identified customer needs

▶▶ **Steps**

Customers are surveyed as to whether their needs are met through competing systems. For this purpose they assign single needs to a prescribed ordinal scale, e.g.:

1 = need is not met by own system / competing system

2 = need is only weakly met by own system / competing system

3 = need is only adequately met by own system / competing system

4 = need is satisfactorily met by own system / competing system

5 = need is very well covered by own system / competing system

The results are entered into a comparative matrix.

DEFINE

Competition Comparison

Competition Comparison					
	1	2	3	4	5
Need 1		○	■ ▲		
Need 2			■	▲	○
Need 3		○	■		▲
Need 4	○			▲	■

Symbols:
Product competitor A = □
Product competitor B = O
Product competitor C = Δ

Goals for the system which is to be developed can be derived from judging which competing system is the best.

MEASURE

ANALYZE

DESIGN

VERIFY

Quality Function Deployment

📁 **Term / Description**

Quality Function Deployment, QFD*, House of Quality

🕑 **When**

In the Measure Phase, specifying customer needs

◎ **Goals**

- Integrated application of customer needs
- Consistent derivation of target values
- Stringent structuring of the development and production process

The QFD target system

Quality	Instrument for planning and developing quality functions based on customer requirements

Function	Quality developments and improvements through the systematic and consistent collaboration of all areas of activity

Deployment	Specification of the required quality into targets for the individual company departments

---

* *QFD was developed between 1967 and 1969 by Yoji Akao and Katsuyo Ishihara to better align product concepts with customer wishes. In 1974 Toyota began to use this tool when introducing new models. From 1981 companies like Ford, Kodak, Hewlett Packard, Xerox, Rockwell, Omark Industries all followed. German industry turned to this tool around 1990.*

▶▶ **Steps**

The first task is to translate the voice of the customer into that of the company.

Goals are then derived in the phases by following clearly defined steps. For each phase an interdisciplinary team provides an integrated view that facilitates planning and decision-making.

A central QFD matrix supports a stringent and structured procedure.

Procedure Model for QFD in DMADV

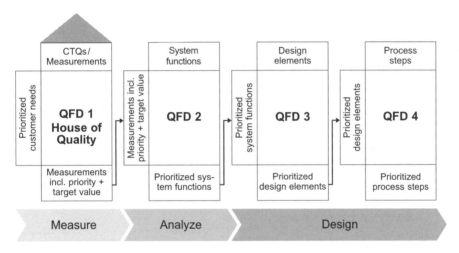

⇒ **Tips**

- The "classical" QFD approach elaborating four Houses of Quality is only rarely applicable and rarely leads directly to success.
- It is important to decide early on if the elaboration of a House of Quality makes sense in the respective project phase.
- The relations matrices should not be too complex.
- The elaboration of a QFD1 and QFD2 is recommended (see the following pages).

DEFINE

MEASURE

ANALYZE

DESIGN

VERIFY

DEFINE

MEASURE

ANALYZE

DESIGN

VERIFY

House of Quality 1

📁 **Term / Description**

Quality Function Deployment 1, QFD 1, House of Quality 1

🕑 **When**

In the Measure Phase, specifying customer needs, prioritizing measurements, determining target values and specifications

◎ **Goals**

– Structured presentation of the relation between customer needs and CTQs using measurements
– Prioritize measurements as basis for further development
– Summarizing presentation of all the information gathered up to this point

▸▸ **Steps**

The "House of Quality" consists of different matrices which are worked out individually. How these are brought together to form a House of Quality will be shown in the following.

Steps for QFD 1

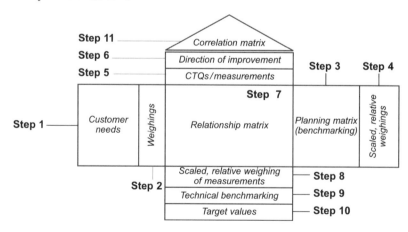

Step 1 (customer needs)
Here the customer needs structured and classified with the aid of the Tree Diagram and the Kano Model are entered. It is important that the customer needs all have the same detailing level. It is recommended to elaborate two Houses of Quality:
1. QFD 1a: Dissatisfier,
2. QFD 1b: Delighter and satisfier.

Step 2 (weighings)
Ensuring that the dissatisfiers are met has greater priority than the delighters and satisfiers. All dissatisfiers have to be met by 100%. The prioritization for delighters and satisfiers undertaken in the AHP are adopted for the House of Quality. No weighings are entered for the House of Quality containing the dissatisfier.

Step 3 und 4 (planning matrix / benchmarking and scaled, relative weighing)
The results of the "customer satisfaction benchmarking" are summarized in the planning matrix. In this benchmarking the customers are asked about the performance of existing systems: is it meeting their needs? Their evaluation follows a scale of 1 (not being met at all) to 5 (need is well met).

The "improvement factor" is derived from this information and it is complimented by the "need priority" of the AHP and a "USP factor". These three factors are corrected by a planning priority so as to obtain an adjusted scaled weighing of customer needs that serves as the basis for the relationship matrix.

Planning Priority

Planning Priority

AHP priority	Improvement factor	USP factor
• Need priorities identified in AHP for satisfier and delighter factors. • Dissatisfiers are always given high priority (100%).	• Takes into consideration the degree of improvement required for the product / process with respect to meeting customer needs (VOC benchmark).	• Takes into consideration a possible differentiation strategy on the basis of an USP. • Are single customer needs to be granted greater attention as USPs?
Comparison **+**	*Comparison* **+**	*Comparison*

= *adjusted scaled, relative weighing (evaluation basis for relationship matrix)*

DEFINE

MEASURE

ANALYZE

DESIGN

VERIFY

105

The planning priority defines the rank order between the single factors within the planning matrix:
- – Need priority (derived from the AHP)
- – Improvement factor (VOC benchmark)
- – USP factor (differentiation based on unique selling proposition)

This distinction is unavoidable because it is always a company-specific decision which factor is to be assigned the most importance in developing the system. The basis for determining the planning priority is an AHP, made up of the three defined factors.

AHP matrix for weighing the factors of the planning priority

Planning Priority	Need priority	Improvement factor	USP factor	Aggregate of the rows	Aggregate scaled
Need priority	1.00	3.00	5.00	1.90	**63.33%**
Improvement factor	0.33	1.00	3.00	0.78	**26.00%**
USP factor	0.20	0.33	1.00	0.32	**10.60%**
Aggregate of the columns	1.53	4.33	9.00	3.00	100.00%

The following scaling is used for evaluation:
1 = equally important
3 = a little more important
5 = more important
7 = much more important
9 = of extremely greater importance

Planning priority		
Need priority [63.33%]	Improvement factor [26%]	USP factor [10.6%]

⇒ **Tip**

The evaluation within the AHP matrix to set the planning priority is be made by the DFSS team in line with the company's strategic orientation.

The "improvement factor" results from the customer evaluation with respect to the satisfaction of single needs. This evaluation is used to define an improvement goal that is assigned to a corresponding improvement factor (see AHP matrix). The improvement factor must be then corrected and adjusted to fit the planning priority.

AHP matrix for scaling the improvement goal

Improvement Goal	5	4	3	2	1	Aggregate of the rows	Scaled aggregate
5	1.00	2.00	3.00	4.00	5.00	1.9471	**38.94%**
4	0.50	1.00	3.00	5.00	5.00	1.5352	**30.70%**
3	0.33	0.33	1.00	3.00	4.00	0.8144	**16.29%**
2	0.25	0.20	0.33	1.00	3.00	0.4487	**8.97%**
1	0.20	0.20	0.25	0.33	1.00	0.2547	**5.09%**
Aggregate of the columns	2.28	3.73	7.58	13.33	18.00	5	100.00%

Scaling for defining the improvement goal:
1 = need is not met by own system / competing system
2 = need is only weakly met by own system / competing system
3 = need is only adequately met by own system / competing system
4 = need is satisfactorily met by own system / competing system
5 = need is very well met by own system / competing system

The weighing corresponding to the improvement goal is entered into the planning matrix.

Identifying the improvement factor

	Benchmark						
	1 (need not met)	2	3 (only adequately met)	4	5 (very well met)	Improvement goal	Improvement goal scaled	Improvement factor
						26.0%		
	A		B		C	0.389	35.0%	9.1%
	A	B	C			0.163	14.6%	3.8%
	A	B	C			0.163	14.6%	3.8%
	A	C				0.090	8.1%	2.1%
			A	B	C	0.307	27.6%	7.2%
						0	0.0%	0.0%
						0	0.0%	0.0%
						0	0.0%	0.0%
						0	0.0%	0.0%
						0	0.0%	0.0%
						1.112	100.0%	26.0%

A = customer viewpoint - current product
B = customer viewpoint - competition
C = improvement goal

In addition to need priority and the improvement factor for a need, the USP factor (Unique Selling Proposition) judges its potential in relation to competing systems. The USP evaluations can also be scaled with the aid of an AHP.

Identifying the USP factor

USP	Strong	Moderate	None	Aggregate of rows	Aggregate scaled
Strong	1.00	2.00	3.00	1.57	**52.47%**
Moderate	0.50	1.00	3.00	1.00	**33.40%**
None	0.33	0.33	1.00	0.42	**14.20%**
Aggregate of columns	1.83	3.33	7.00	3.00	100.00%

For every customer need there is, as the result of the planning matrix, an adjusted scaled priority that contains the corrected factors follows: need priority, improvement factor, and USP factor. This priority forms in turn the evaluation basis for the further steps in the relationship matrix.

Planning Matrix
Example: passenger seat

Customer need	Weighing (AHP)	Need priorities in total	1 (need not met)	2	3 (only adequately met)	4	5 (very well met)	Improvement goal	Improvement goal scaled	Improvement factor in total	USP	Improvement goal	Improvement goal scaled	USP factor in total	Adjusted scaled priority	Ranking
		63.33%			26.0%								10.6%			
I'd like the seats to be more robust against vandalism.	29.19%	18.5%	A		B	C		0.307	23.1%	6.0%	Moderate	0.334	18.0%	1.9%	26.41%	2
I would like a seat whose parts cannot be stolen.	41.33%	26.2%		A	B	C		0.389	29.3%	7.6%	High	0.525	28.2%	3.0%	36.80%	1
I'd like the seat to be easily installed and dismantled	17.72%	11.2%	A	B		C		0.307	23.1%	6.0%	High	0.525	28.2%	3.0%	20.24%	3
I would like the seats to always look clean.	4.64%	2.9%	A	B	C			0.163	12.3%	3.2%	Moderate	0.334	18.0%	1.9%	8.04%	5
I would like the seats to be easily cleanable.	7.12%	4.5%	A	B	C			0.163	12.3%	3.2%	None	0.142	7.6%	0.8%	8.51%	4
		0.0%						0	0.0%	0.0%		0	0.0%	0.0%	0.0%	6
		0.0%						0	0.0%	0.0%		0	0.0%	0.0%	0.0%	6
		0.0%						0	0.0%	0.0%		0	0.0%	0.0%	0.0%	6
		0.0%						0	0.0%	0.0%		0	0.0%	0.0%	0.0%	6
		0.0%						0	0.0%	0.0%		0	0.0%	0.0%	0.0%	6
		63.3%						1.329	100.0%	26.0%		1.858	100.0%	10.6%	100.0%	

Benchmark — *USP*

Overall Priority

Customer needs with AHP weighing

Scaled priorities compared to overall priority

Adjusted, scaled priority with corresponding ranking

The customer need – "I would like the seat to be easily installed and dismantled" – is evaluated with 17.72 % in the AHP matrix. Both the aimed-at improvement goal as well as the strategy to meet the need as an USP vis-à-vis competing systems, lead to an adjusted scaled priority of 20.24 %. This priority now represents the basis for evaluating the relevant measurements in the relationship matrix.

Step 5 (CTQs and measurements)
CTQs and measurements are identified with the aid of the transformation table and are listed here.

DEFINE

MEASURE

ANALYZE

DESIGN

VERIFY

DEFINE

MEASURE

ANALYZE

DESIGN

VERIFY

Step 6 (improvement direction)
The improvement direction is fixed and given a symbol for each listed measurement.

Improvement Direction

↑	1	Maximize
O	0	Meet exactly so
↓	-1	Minimize

Step 7 (relationship matrix)
The relationships between the prioritized customer needs and the measurements are formed in this matrix. Because the measurements are derived directly from the customer needs, each correlates strongly with at least one need. The goal is to identify at least one strong relationship with a measurement for each need.

The market expertise and technological know-how of the team members is decisive for answering the following questions:
- To what extent do the measurements indicate the degree of fulfillment of the respective need?
- To what extent does a positive change of the measurement (based on the envisioned improvement direction) lead to a better fulfillment of the respective need?

A scale is used for the degree of the correlation.

Correlation scale between measurement and customer need

Symbol	Meaning	Number
/	No correlation	0
△	Possible correlation	1
O	Moderate correlation	3
◉	Strong correlation	9

Incorrect evaluations in the relationship matrix have far-reaching repercussions on the project results. Any uncertainty about evaluation must be taken seriously! One very helpful strategy is to formulate an operational definition for the measurements (what is to be measured with which method?). Strive for consensus in the evaluations, not objectivity! It is unadvisable to look for compromises as a way of shortening the procedure.

Step 8 (scaled, relative weighing of measurements)
The scaled, relative weighing of the measurements enables the recognition of the focal points for the subsequent system development. The weighing of a measurement is calculated from the aggregate product of the correlation number and the overall priority.

Relationship matrix with scaled, relative weighing of measurements

Example: passenger seat

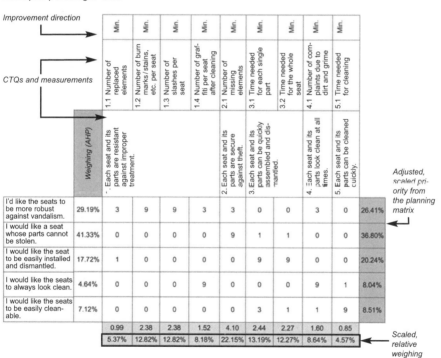

Improvement direction →	Weighing (AHP)	1.1 Number of replaced elements	1.2 Number of burn marks/stains, etc. per seat	1.3 Number of slashes per seat	1.4 Number of graffiti per seat after cleaning	2.1 Number of missing elements	3.1 Time needed for each single part	3.2 Time needed for the whole seat	4.1 Number of complaints due to dirt and grime	5.1 Time needed for cleaning	Adjusted, scaled priority from the planning matrix
		Min.	Min.	Min.	Min.	Min.	Min.	Min.	Min.	Min.	
		1. Each seat and its parts are resistant against improper treatment.				2. Each seat and its parts are secure against theft.	3. Each seat and its parts can be quickly assembled and dismantled.		4. Each seat and its parts look clean at all times.	5. Each seat and its parts can be cleaned quickly.	
I'd like the seats to be more robust against vandalism.	29.19%	3	9	9	3	3	0	0	3	0	26.41%
I would like a seat whose parts cannot be stolen.	41.33%	0	0	0	0	9	1	1	0	0	36.80%
I would like the seat to be easily installed and dismantled.	17.72%	1	0	0	0	0	9	9	0	0	20.24%
I would like the seats to always look clean.	4.64%	0	0	0	9	0	0	0	9	1	8.04%
I would like the seats to be easily cleanable.	7.12%	0	0	0	0	0	3	1	1	9	8.51%
		0.99	2.38	2.38	1.52	4.10	2.44	2.27	1.60	0.85	
		5.37%	12.82%	12.82%	8.18%	22.15%	13.19%	12.27%	8.64%	4.57%	

CTQs and measurements

Scaled, relative weighing

DEFINE

MEASURE

ANALYZE

DESIGN

VERIFY

Step 9 and 10 (technological benchmarking and target values)
Technological benchmarking identifies the current performance capability of one's own system and competing systems with regard to the prioritized measurements.

For each measurement the present system in place (A) is compared and evaluated with the competing system (B). Depending on the target level (C) of the CTQs, specific target values and tolerances (USL / LSL) can be derived for the individual measurements.

Another possibility is to supplement technological benchmarking with the degree of difficulty involved in attaining a goal. The relevant question is: how great is the effort / input to attain the set goal or how difficult is it to achieve the goal?

The degree of difficulty is assessed on a scale of 1 (very simple attainment) to 5 (very difficult attainment). By multiplying the weighing of the respective measurement a gauge is generated for assessing the risk of realization. This shows which measurements are the most critical for realizing the project.

Specifying Customer Needs

DEFINE

MEASURE

ANALYZE

DESIGN

VERIFY

Technological benchmarking and target values with tolerances

Example: passenger seat

	1.1 Number of replaced elements	1.2 Number of burn marks/stains, etc. per seat	1.3 Number of slashes per seat	1.4 Number of graffiti per seat after cleaning	2.1 Number of missing elements	3.1 Time needed for each single part	3.2 Time needed for the whole seat	4.1 Number of complaints due to dirt and grime	5.1 Time needed for cleaning		
	Min.	Min.	Min.	Min.	Min.	Min.	Min.	Min.	Min.		**Measurements**
	5.37%	12.82%	12.82%	8.18%	22.15%	13.19%	12.27%	8.64%	4.57%	0%	Scaled weighings
	No./month and seat	No. of new units/month	No. new units/month	No. new units/month	No. new units/month	Minutes/seat	Minutes/seat	No./month	Minutes/seat		Unit
	Discrete	Discrete	Discrete	Discrete	Discrete	Continuous	Continuous	Discrete	Continuous		Data type
	0	0	0	0	0	5	10	1	2		Target value
	0	0	0	0	0	0	0	0	0		LSL
	0	0	0	0	0	8	12	0	4		USL
											Quality key figure
5		C	C		C	C		C			
4	C	B		C			C		C		Technological benchmark
3	B		B	B	B	B		B			
2	A	A		A		A	B		B		
1			A		A		A	A	A		
Optional	2	4	5	3	5	5	4	1	4		Degree of difficulty
	10.73%	51.30%	64.12%	24.53%	110.73%	65.95%	49.08	8.64%	18.26%	0.0%	Critical features for attaining goal
	8	4	3	6	1	2	5	9	7	10	Ranking

DEFINE

MEASURE

ANALYZE

DESIGN

VERIFY

Step 11 (correlation matrix)

The correlation matrix helps to identify dependencies between measurements. In particular conflicts are to be pinpointed which must be solved innovatively in the subsequent system development. One simple example is increasing the stability of an object, whereby this step runs counter to another goal, to reduce the weigh of the same object. The measurements with their respective improvement direction are compared.

Correlation Matrix

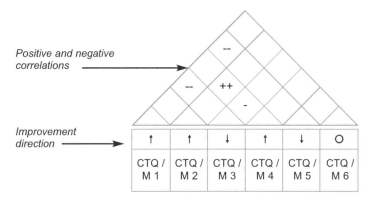

Positive and negative correlations

Improvement direction

| CTQ / M 1 | CTQ / M 2 | CTQ / M 3 | CTQ / M 4 | CTQ / M 5 | CTQ / M 6 |

Correlation symbols:
- ++ Strongly positive effect
- + Slightly positive effect
- O No effect
- - Slightly negative effect
- -- Strongly negative effect
- M Measurement

Improvement direction:
- ↑ Must be increased
- O Must remain constant
- ↓ Must be reduced

The correlation roof only represents positive and negative interactions between the measurements. The corresponding interaction can be considered and investigated, however, via the degree of difficulty (step 9 "technological benchmarking"). The negative interactions shown in the correlation roof can be formulated as technological conflicts / contradictions. Methods for solving such conflicts will be presented in the Analyze Phase.

Correlation Matrix

Example: passenger seat

Correlation Matrix / Improvement direction	Improvement direction	1.1 Number of replaced elements (Min.)	1.2 Number of burn marks/stains, etc. per seat (Min.)	1.3 Number of slashes per seat (Min.)	1.4 Number of graffiti per seat after cleaning (Min.)	2.1 Number of missing parts (Min.)	3.1 Time needed for each single part (Min.)	3.2 Time needed for the whole seat (Min.)	4.1 Number of complaints due to dirt and grime (Min.)	5.1 Time needed for cleaning (Min.)
1.1 Number of replaced elements	Min.		++	++	+	++				
1.2 Number of burn marks/stains, etc. per seat	Min.	++							+	
1.3 Number of slashes per seat	Min.	++								
1.4 Number of graffiti per seat after cleaning	Min.	+								
2.1 Number of missing parts	Min.						−			
3.1 Time needed for each single part	Min.					−				
3.2 Time needed for the whole seat	Min.									
4.1 Number of complaints due to dirt and grime	Min.	+								
5.1 Time needed for cleaning	Min.									

↑ Measurements   ↑ Improvement direction

- The team identifies a negative interaction between the measurements for:
  - the assembly time for single parts and
  - number of missing parts.
- If the assembly time is to be reduced, which is demanded by the improvement direction, theft-proof design can no longer be guaranteed.
- This negative correlation has to be considered as the project proceeds; the team resolves to look at the technological conflict with TRIZ.

DEFINE

MEASURE

ANALYZE

DESIGN

VERIFY

Design Scorecard

☐ Term / Description
Design scorecard

🕑 When
In the Measure Phase, specifying customer needs, then in Analyze, Design, Verify

◎ Goal
Summarize the measurements and their specifications

▸▸ Steps
The target values and tolerances of the measurements are described in a table. These details are supplemented with further information, such as the operational definition and the quality key figures.

Design Scorecard
Example: passenger seat

Design Scorecard											
No.	Measurement	Unit	Operational Definition	LSL	USL	Mean	StDev	D	U	O	DPMO
1.1	No. replaced single parts	No. / month & seat									
1.2	No. burn marks & stains	No. replaced seats / month									
1.3	No. slashes	No. replaced seats / month									
1.4	No. missing parts	No. / month									
1.5	No. missing parts	(Qualitative)									
1.6	Assembly time parts	Min.									
1.7	Assembly time seat	Min.									
1.8	No. complaints	Complaints / month									
1.9	Cleaning time seat	Min. / seat									
1.10											

116

Risk Evaluation

📁 **Term / Description**

Risk evaluation

🕐 **When**

In the Measure Phase, specifying customer needs, evaluating risks

◎ **Goal**

Evaluate the risks which can emerge when important CTQs are not met

▶▶ **Steps**

The team estimates how complex it is realize technologically the measure-ments' target values and what effects are triggered if these targets are not met:

Possible effects if target values are not met

Possible effects for the customer	*Possible internal effect*
• Raises the variation of product qualities • Raises the probability that the product does not function properly • Delays delivery times • Raises the product price • Decreases benefit / value • Increases rework	• Increases rework, production costs • Reduces profit • Poor customer relations • Loss of customers • Loss of growth opportunities • Poor reputation in the marketplace • Raises the barriers of entering into other markets

The risks are documented in a risk evaluation matrix.

A risk evaluation matrix is presented on the following page.

DEFINE

MEASURE

ANALYZE

DESIGN

VERIFY

117

Risk evaluation matrix

			Design Scorecard											
No.	Measurement	Unit	Operational Definition	LSL	USL	Mean	StDev	D	U	O	DPMO	Effect with non-fulfill-ment	Expected diffi-culty in realiz-ation	Remarks
1.1	No. replaced single parts	No./month & seat												
1.2	No. burn marks & stains	No. replaced seats/month												
1.3	No. slashes	No. replaced seats/month												
1.4	No. missing parts	No./month												
1.5	No. missing parts	(Qualitative)												
1.6	Assembly time parts	Min.												
1.7	Assembly time seat	Min.												
1.8	No. complaints	Complaints/month												
1.9	Cleaning time seat	Min./seat												
1.10														

Quality Key Figures

📁 **Term / Description**

Quality Key Figures, Process Performance

🕐 **When**

At the conclusion of the Measure Phase, continuously during Analyze and Design, and in particular in Verify

◎ **Goals**

- Determine the performance capability of a process in terms of customer requirements
- Describe the status quo and the improvements after implementing solutions

▶▶ **Steps**

The quality key figures measuring performance quality in Six Sigma[+Lean] are:

DPMO	Defects Per Million Opportunities
ppm	Parts per Million
DPU	Defects Per Unit
Yield	Yield
C_p and C_{pk}	Process capability indexes
Process Sigma	Sigma value

DEFINE

MEASURE

ANALYZE

DESIGN

VERIFY

Parts per Million (ppm)

☐ **Term / Description**

Parts per Million (ppm)

🕓 **When**

In the Measure Phase, specifying customer needs, then in Analyze, Design, Verify

◎ **Goal**

Focus on the customer viewpoint: a unit with one defect and a part with several defects are equally defective and are counted as a defect – because the unit, although with only one defect, is of no use to the customer.

▶▶ **Steps**

– Determine the defect opportunities for a part / unit which result in its characterization as defective.
– Determine the number of examined parts / units and count the defective / faulty units.
– Calculate the ppm value:

$$\text{ppm} = \frac{\text{no. of defective units}}{\text{no. of units in total}} \cdot 1{,}000{,}000$$

⇨ **Tip**

If there is only one defect opportunity the DMPO value matches the ppm value.

ppm

Example: spray-painting process, parts per million

- From a total of 80 jobs 63 either required rework due to defective paint application or were not completed on time:

$$\text{ppm} = \frac{63}{80} \cdot 1{,}000{,}000 = 787{,}500$$

- The ppm rate is 787,500.

Defects per Unit (DPU)

📇 **Term / Description**

Defects per Unit (DPU)

🕐 **When**

In the Measure Phase, specifying customer needs, then in Analyze, Design, Verify

◎ **Goal**

Determine the average number of defects per unit

▸▸ **Steps**

- Define the defects (every defect opportunity of a unit is a defect)
- Determine the number of investigated units and count the defects
- Calculate the DPU value:

$$DPU = \frac{no.\ of\ defects\ in\ total}{no.\ of\ units\ in\ total}$$

⇨ **Tip**

Taken together, the three quality key figures DPMO, ppm, and DPU provide a comprehensive picture of process performance – it is therefore strongly recommended to use all three key figures.

DPU

Example: spray-painting process, defects per unit

- From 80 jobs 108 defects were identified:

$$DPU = \frac{108}{80} = 1.35$$

- The DPU rate is 1.35. This means that a produced or worked unit has on average 1.35 defects.

DEFINE

MEASURE

ANALYZE

DESIGN

VERIFY

121

Yield

☐ Term / Description
Yield

🕘 When
In the Measure Phase, specifying customer needs, then in Analyze, Design, Verify

◎ Goal
Determine the share of non-defective units or the yield of a process

▸▸ Steps
- **Yield:** reflects the share of good, non-defective units

$$Y = \frac{\text{no. of non-defective units}}{\text{no. of units in total}}$$

    – Connection between DPO and yield:

$$Y = 1 - DPO \text{ whereby } DPO = \frac{D}{N \cdot O}$$

- **Rolled Throughput Yield:** this identifies the probability that a unit passes through the whole process without becoming defective. This total yield is calculated from the product of the individual sub-process yields.

$$Y_{RTP} = Y_{Sub1} \cdot Y_{Sub2} \cdot \ldots \cdot Y_{Subn}$$

- **Normalized Yield:** shows the average yield per process step. *Attention:* this measurement can be misleading when the yields of the individual process steps differ strongly from one another.

$$Y_{Norm} = \sqrt[n]{Y_{RTP}}$$

122

⇾ **Tips**
- Two characteristics can be distinguished in yield:
  1. The relationship between non-defective units and units in total (yield in classical production).
  2. The relationship between the produced yield to deployed amount (yield in chemical/pharmaceutical industry).
- The Yield is usually determined before possible rework occurs (First Pass Yield.

Yield

Example 1: spray-painting process – yield

- From 80 paint applications only 21 were without defects.
- The yield rate is thus 26.25%.

$$\text{Yield} = \frac{21}{80} = 0.2625 = 26.25\%$$

Example 2: spray-painting process – rolled throughput yield

- The following yields were calculated for the individual process steps:

$$Y_1 = 92\% \rightarrow Y_2 = 82\% \rightarrow Y_3 = 84\% \rightarrow Y_4 = 82\% \rightarrow Y_5 = 95\%$$

- The probability that a unit can pass through the whole process without becoming defective is:

$$Y_{RTP} = 0.92 \cdot 0.82 \cdot 0.84 \cdot 0.82 \cdot 0.95 \cong 0.494$$

DEFINE

MEASURE

ANALYZE

DESIGN

VERIFY

123

DEFINE

MEASURE

ANALYZE

DESIGN

VERIFY

C_p and C_{pk}-values

☐ Term/Description
C_p and C_{pk}

☼ When
In the Measure Phase, specifying customer needs, then in Analyze, Design, Verify

◎ Goals
- Ascertain the relationship between the customer specification limits (tolerance) and natural spread of the process (C_p-value).
- Determine the centering of the process (C_{pk}-value).

▶ Steps

C_p-value:
- Determine upper and lower specification limits.
- Divide the distance between the upper and lower specification limits (tolerance) by the 6-point standard deviation.
- If the data is not in normal distribution: divide the tolerance by the percentile distance of ± 3 standard deviations (corresponds to 99.73%).

With normal distribution	With non-normal distribution
$C_p = \dfrac{USL - LSL}{6s}$	$C_p = \dfrac{USL - LSL}{x_{0.99865} - x_{0.00135}}$

C_{pk}-value:
- Divide the distance between the closest specification limit and the mean by the 3-point standard deviation of the process. This takes into consideration the position of the process.
- If the data is not in normal distribution: divide the distance between the closest specification limit and the median by the half-percentile distance.

With normal distribution	With non-normal distribution
$C_{pk} = \min\left[\dfrac{USL - \bar{x}}{3s}; \dfrac{\bar{x} - LSL}{3s}\right]$	$C_{pk} = \min\left[\dfrac{USL - x_{0.5}}{x_{0.99865} - x_{0.5}}; \dfrac{x_{0.5} - LSL}{x_{0.5} - x_{0.00135}}\right]$

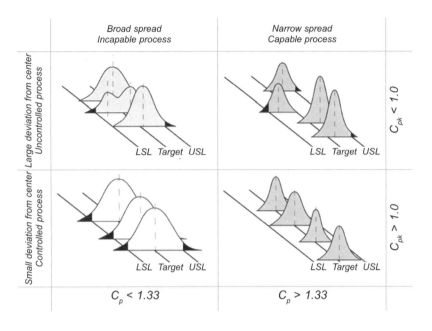

⇨ **Tips**

- A high C_p-value is a necessary but not a sufficient condition for a good process Sigma value. A high process Sigma value can only be first achieved when the process centering is taken into consideration, i.e. a good C_{pk}-value.

- To achieve a Sigma value of 6 (a Six Sigma process) the C_p and C_{pk} must assume the value of 2 (at least 6 standard deviations fit in between the mean and the customer specification limits). Due to the assumed process shifts of 1.5 standard deviations, Six Sigma corporations like Motorola have set C_p-values of 2 and C_{pk}-values of 1.5 as their goals.

- In case of a long term observation the C_p and C_{pk}-values are signified as P_p and P_{pk}.

DEFINE

MEASURE

ANALYZE

DESIGN

VERIFY

Example of C_p, C_{pk}-values

For spray-painting operations the specification limits are set as follows:
LSL = 100 and USL = 180. The collected data showed a mean of 154.4 and
a standard deviation of 22.86. The data is in normal distribution.

$$C_p = \frac{USL - LSL}{6s} = \frac{180 - 100}{6 \cdot 22.86} = 0.58$$

$$C_{pk} = \min \left[\frac{USL - \bar{x}}{3s} ; \frac{\bar{x} - LSL}{3s} \right] = \min \left[\frac{180 - 154.54}{68.58} ; \frac{154.54 - 100}{68.58} \right] = \min \left[0.37; 0.79 \right] = 0.37$$

Example: C_p and C_{pk} in Minitab®

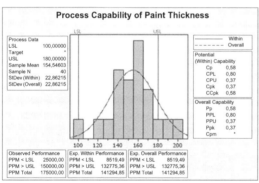

Graph result:
the upper and lower specification limits
and a few statistical indicators from the
sample:
the histogram shows how the data lies
in relationship to the specification limits.
The curve depicts the normal distribution, taking into consideration the short-
and long-term observation. This example
does not take this distinction into account.

The C_p and C_{pk}-values: the greater the
values the more capable the process.
$C_p = 2$ and $C_{pk} = 1.5$ matches a Six Sigma
level.

The short- and long-term process capability is identical because no subgroups
are given.

DEFINE

Process Sigma

📁 **Term / Description**

Process Sigma, Sigma value

🕐 **When**

In the Measure Phase, specifying customer needs, Analyze, Design, Verify

◎ **Goals**

– Depict the performance capability of a process, especially in relation to the specification limits
– Utilize as benchmark and / or best-practice

▶▶ **Steps**

– Via **DPMO**
Identify from the Sigma conversion table (see appendix).

– Via **Yield**
Identify from the Sigma conversion table using first-pass yield.

– Via **z-transformation**
Identify solely with normally distributed, continuous data.

MEASURE

ANALYZE

DESIGN

VERIFY

Z-Method for Calculating Sigma

Prerequisite: continuous data in normal distribution

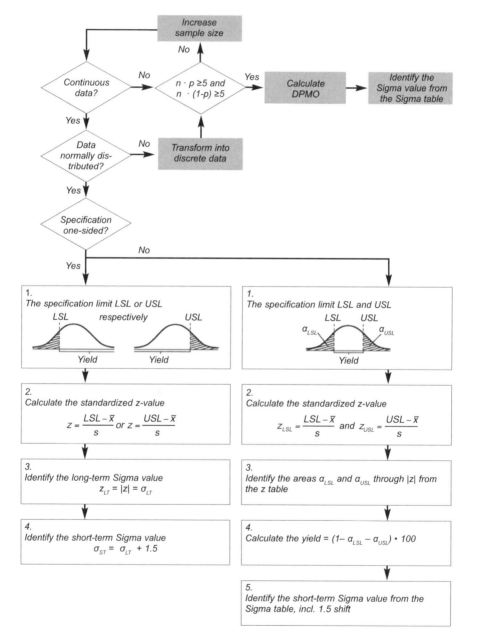

⇨ **Tip**

Do not impose the Sigma value as the sole performance indicator. Utilize those values and indicators which customers and employees understand and accept.

Z-method for Sigma calculation
Example: two-sided CTQ

- Our customer asks for delivery 7 days at the earliest after placing the order, but no later than 20 days. The standard deviation is 4 days.

- We have $z_{USL} = \dfrac{20 - 13.5}{4} = 1.625$ and $z_{LSL} = \dfrac{7 - 13.5}{4} = -1.625$

- From the z-table we obtain $\alpha_{USL} = 0.0516$ and $\alpha_{LSL} = 0.0516$

- Yield = $(1 - 0.0516 - 0.0516) \cdot 100\% = 89.68\%$

- $s_{ST} = 2.75$

- $s_{LT} = 2.75 - 1.5 = 1.25$

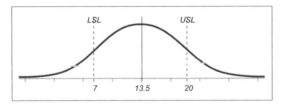

DEFINE

MEASURE

ANALYZE

DESIGN

VERIFY

Gate Review

☐ Term / Description
Gate Review, phase check, phase assessment

☉ When
At the conclusion of each phase

◎ Goals
- Inform the Sponsor about the results and measures taken in the respective phases
- Assess the results
- Decide on the further course of the project

▶▶ Steps
The results are presented in full and in an easily comprehensible form. The Sponsor is to examine the status of the project on the basis of the following criteria:
- Results are complete,
- Probability of project success,
- Resources are optimally allocated in the project.

The Sponsor decides if the project can enter the next phase.

The results from the Measure Phase are presented to the Sponsor and Stakeholders in the Gate Review. The following questions need to be answered in a complete and comprehensible presentation:

DEFINE

MEASURE

ANALYZE

DESIGN

VERIFY

Selecting customers:
- How was the target market determined?
- How were the target customers of the product/process identified? What characterizes them?
- Were the target customers segmented? Which target customers have which priority?

Collecting customer voices:
- Which surveying methods were selected? What were the results?
- How was the Customer Interaction Study carried out? What were the results?
- Are the permitted target costs identified? In which price range can the product/process be offered?

Specifying customer needs:
- What are the customer needs? How are they related?
- Are there contradictory customer needs and how were these taken into account?
- Are there competing systems and if so how do they fulfill customer needs?
- Have the customer voices been transformed into CTQs and measurements? What are the priorities?
- Was a technological benchmarking carried out? If yes, how? What are the results?
- How were the target values and tolerances for the measurements determined?
- Which defect rates may the measurements show?
- Are there conflicts to be expected in fulfilling individual CTQs/ measurements?
- Which limitations and obstacles were identified?
- What consequences are to be expected if the CTQs are not met?

On managing the project:
- Does it make sense to proceed with the project?
- Has the Business Case been altered in line with the new information and insights?
- Which lessons have been learned in the Measure Phase and what kinds of steps do they require?

Design for Six Sigma^{+Lean} Toolset

Toolset

ANALYZE

DEFINE

MEASURE

ANALYZE

DESIGN

VERIFY

Phase 3: Analyze

Goals

– Identify and prioritize system functions
– Develop and optimize a design concept
– Examine this design concept as to its capacity to meet customer requirements

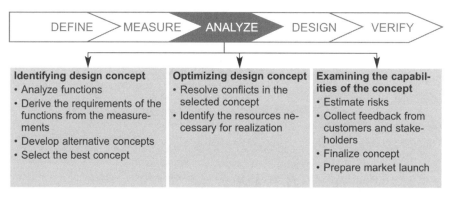

Identifying design concept	Optimizing design concept	Examining the capabilities of the concept
• Analyze functions • Derive the requirements of the functions from the measurements • Develop alternative concepts • Select the best concept	• Resolve conflicts in the selected concept • Identify the resources necessary for realization	• Estimate risks • Collect feedback from customers and stakeholders • Finalize concept • Prepare market launch

Steps

After the requirements are established, the design concepts can now be developed and the best selected. Contradictions in the concepts are resolved and the critical process and input variables are defined.

A roadmap for the Analyze Phase is presented on the opposite page.

Most Important Tools

- Function Analysis
- Transfer Function
- QFD 2
- Creativity Techniques
- Ishikawa Diagram
- TRIZ
- Benchmarking
- Pugh Matrix
- FMEA

- Anticipatory Failure Detection
- Design Scorecards
- Prototyping

Analyze Roadmap

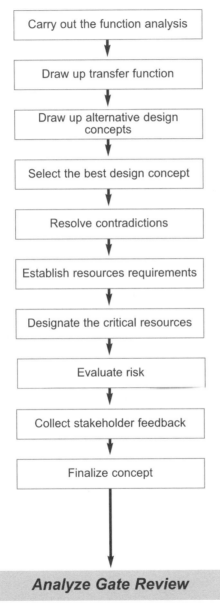

Carry out the function analysis

↓

Draw up transfer function

↓

Draw up alternative design concepts

↓

Select the best design concept

↓

Resolve contradictions

↓

Establish resources requirements

↓

Designate the critical resources

↓

Evaluate risk

↓

Collect stakeholder feedback

↓

Finalize concept

↓

Analyze Gate Review

Sponsor: Go / No-go Decision

DEFINE

MEASURE

ANALYZE

DESIGN

VERIFY

DEFINE

MEASURE

ANALYZE

DESIGN

VERIFY

Identifying Design Concept

📁 **Term / Description**

Design Concept Identification

🕐 **When**

In the Analyze Phase, identifying alternative design concepts

◎ **Goals**

– Develop alternative design concepts on the basis of prioritized functions
– Identify the best concept under consideration of the defined customer requirements

▸▸ **Steps**

With regard to the functions of a system several alternative concepts are always conceivable for its development.

From the possibilities the concept is selected that meets the CTQs and CTBs (critical to business) best. The development of the concept begins with setting out the basic concept and ends with a definition of the detailed characteristics in a detailed concept.

The level of detail increases continually. The level of detail where a basic concept can be frozen (the conclusion of the Analyze Phase) is always project specific and should be set by the project team when launching the Analyze Phase.

From the basic concept to detailed concept

Step 1:
Basic concept or high-level concept

Step 2:
Detailed concept or detailed design

Level of detail

Low   High

Anayze Phase   **Design Phase**

The prerequisite for the development of alternative concepts is initially an exact analysis of all system functions. The abstract formulation of the system functions – without any solutions – is the basis for creative concept ideas.

DEFINE

MEASURE

ANALYZE

DESIGN

VERIFY

Analyzing Functions

📁 **Term / Description**
Functional Analysis, analyzing and elaborating system functions

🕙 **When**
In the Analyze Phase, identifying the design concept, analyzing functions

◎ **Goals**
– Describe the system – without solutions – as a system of effects made up of interacting functions
– Identify and prioritize all relevant sub-functions within this system

▶▶ **Steps**
The effects of a system are based on its attributes, its application, and its relevant importance.
Accordingly, the functions generating these effects can be subdivided into three categories.

Function categories according to type of effect

Object function (passive)	Performance function (active)	Prestige function
Concerns the system itself	Concerns the use of the system	Concerns the importance of the system
E.g.: Taking up an object (chair, seat, table, etc.)	E.g.: Simple ergonomic handling	E.g.: Attractive design
	E.g.: Removal of plaque (teeth)	E.g.: Easily recognizable employees through special uniforms

As depicted in the table a function should be formulated concisely and clearly. In addition, every function can be classified according to its mode of action:
- Useful functions
- Harmful functions

Depicting and analyzing the function reveals the contradictions and connections between the functions.
(See the function example)

DEFINE

MEASURE

ANALYZE

DESIGN

VERIFY

Depicting Functions

📁 **Term / Description**

Functional Analysis

🕒 **When**

In the Analyze Phase, identifying the design concept

◎ **Goals**

– Graphic description of all cause-effect relations between the involved system components and their functions
– Systematically analyze useful as well as harmful or insufficient or super-fluous relationships
– Identify conflicts and contradictions

▶▶ **Steps**

The system and its effect environment are broken down into single elements and are designated in corresponding nouns. Their respective effect or function is described in verb form.

A distinction is drawn between the following basic functional terms:
– Useful functions
– Harmful functions

Cause-Effect Relationships

Symbols for depicting elements and functions

Elements	
Components	Components
Super system	Elements of the Super system
Product	Product

Functions	
———▶	Useful normal function
+++++▶	Useful insufficient function
———▶	Useful excessive function
▪▪▪▪▪▶	Useful function with parameters
═══▶	Harmful function
▪▪▪▪▪▶	Harmful function with parameters

DEFINE

Depicting Functions
Example: super system motor vehicle

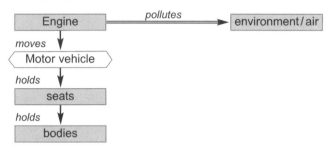

Depicting Functions
Example: super system "toothbrush"

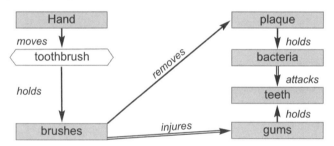

MEASURE

ANALYZE

Tips
- When a process is developed the five to seven identified process steps (verb + noun) on a SIPOC level correspond to functions.
- The conflicts and contradictions evident in the depiction can be analyzed and eliminated with the aid of the TRIZ method.
- When developing materials the functions are frequently equated with the attributes of a material, e.g.:
  - Electrical resistance (conducting a current),
  - Stability (bear mechanical strain).
- The connection between the identified and described functions and CTQs / measurements characterizes the system's mode of action when interacting with the customers. This connection is also known as the transfer function.

DESIGN

VERIFY

DEFINE

MEASURE

ANALYZE

DESIGN

VERIFY

Deriving Requirements to Functions

📁 **Term / Description**

Quality Function Deployment 2, QFD 2, House of Quality 2

🕑 **When**

In the Analyze Phase, identifying the design concept

◎ **Goals**

– Elaborate the transfer functions which show the connection between the identified system functions and the measurements
– Prioritize the functions, taking into consideration the prioritized measurements

▶▶ **Steps**

The relation between the identified functions and the weighed measurements are identified within QFD 2:

QFD 2

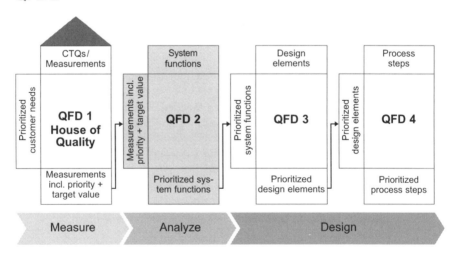

The influence of the system functions on the individual measurements is analyzed first of all.

Here the following questions must be answered:
1. Are all the system functions identified which contribute to meeting the measurements?
2. How strongly does a system function influence the respective measurement?

The connection between CTQs/measurements and the system functions can be depicted with the aid of QFD 2. This is also known as the transfer function.

QFD 2

Generic example

	System functions				Scaled, relative weighing M
	F 1	F 2	F 3		
Measurement 1	◉				25%
Measurement 2	○	◉			45%
Measurement 3		△	◉		30%
Weighing (absolute)	3.6	4.35	2.7	10.65	100%
Scaled, relative weighing	33.8%	40.8%	25.4%	100%	

Legend for evaluating the cause-effect relation:

Symbol	Meaning	Number
╱	No correlation	0
△	Possible correlation	1
○	Moderate correlation	3
◉	Strong correlation	9
M	Measurement	
F	Function	

The overall priority of the measurements derived in the Measure Phase is taken into consideration when determining the weighing of the system functions. This weighing helps to set priorities for further concept development.

Besides QFD 2 other methods can be used to derive transfer functions.

Transfer functions are presented on the following page.

DEFINE

MEASURE

ANALYZE

DESIGN

VERIFY

DEFINE

MEASURE

ANALYZE

DESIGN

VERIFY

Transfer Functions

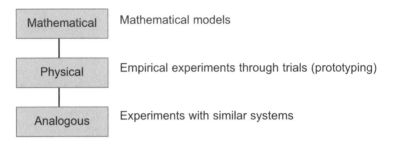

Mathematical	Mathematical models
Physical	Empirical experiments through trials (prototyping)
Analogous	Experiments with similar systems

Ideally the connection between the measurement and the sub-functions can be described as a mathematical function:

Transfer Function
Examples

Tenability of a system	Tenability system = $\min_{i=1}^{n}$ [tenability system components]
Maximum lead time of a serial process with 95% probability	Max. PLT = $\sum$ average PLT process step + 1.96 x standard deviation of the process step
Average lead time of a process	Average PLT = $\sum$ average PLT single process steps

⇨ **Tips**
- Not all of the identified system functions influence all measurements.
- Ideally all functions are "decoupled", i.e. system functions are completely independent of one another and each has a direct influence on exactly one measurement.

144

Developing Alternative Concepts

📁 **Term/Description**

Developing alternative concepts by taking into consideration system functions

🕑 **When**

In the Analyze Phase, identifying design concepts

◎ **Goal**

Generate alternative concept ideas to realize the system functions

▶▶ **Steps**

The concept to be developed is to fulfill the identified and prioritized functions in the best possible way.

There are many methods which can be used to develop creative concept ideas. Some methods are presented in the following:

– Creativity techniques like:
   - Brainstorming
   - Brain Writing
   - Mind Mapping
   - SCAMPER
   - Morphological box
– Benchmarking
– TRIZ

⇨ **Tips**

• The complexity level of the system which is to be developed determines the procedure and its steps. If the complexity level is high, sub-concepts for the individual functions should be developed first. These are then merged and result in an overall concept for the system.
• The developed alternative design concepts are to be documented in a clear and structured form. A combination of documented descriptions in writing and supplementary sketches helps the team later to select the optimal concept.

DEFINE

MEASURE

ANALYZE

DESIGN

VERIFY

Brainstorming

☐ **Term / Description**
Brainstorming, creativity technique for structuring and evaluating a collection of ideas

🕑 **When**
In the Analyze Phase, developing alternative concepts

◎ **Goal**
Develop concept ideas on the basis of the system functions

▸▸ **Steps**
Brainstorming leads to a collection of ideas which is as diverse and extensive as possible. The following brainstorming rules guarantee a strict separation of ideas:

Brainstorming rules:
1. Each proposal counts
2. No discussion about the proposals
3. No "killer phrases" allowed
4. No explanations when collecting ideas
5. All participants in the session are to be involved
6. Let others finish and listen

A brainstorming session is to proceed as follows:
1. Formulate and document the rules, pin them up in the room
2. Set out and write down the theme or goal
3. Collect ideas (actual brainstorming): 3 - 5 minutes
4. Explain and structure the ideas (affinity diagram)
5. Derive and visualize criteria
6. Evaluate collected ideas on the basis of the criteria
7. Select the "good" ideas and pursue them further

Brainstorming can be structured with the help of an Ishikawa diagram.

Ishikawa Diagram for Brainstorming
Example: passenger seat

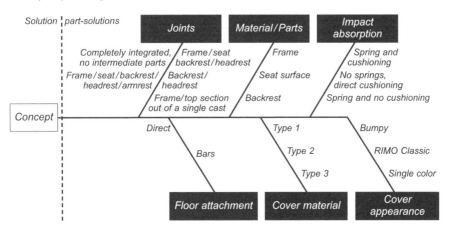

⇒ **Tips**

- The labels given to the "fish bones" (design elements of the system – process and input variables) can be adjusted individually in the Ishikawa Diagram. It is important that the whole system is considered.
- The diagram structures brainstorming, makes it easier to generate ideas and serves as an ideal basis for further pursuing concept ideas.

DEFINE

MEASURE

ANALYZE

DESIGN

VERIFY

Brain Writing

☐ Term / Description
Creativity technique, structured idea collection and evaluation

☉ When
In the Analyze and Design Phases, developing alternative concepts

◎ Goal
Concentrated generation of alternative concept ideas

►► Steps
Brain Writing is used whenever – due to the complex thematic – it seems to make sense to collect ideas in a calmer, concentrated atmosphere or when persons involved are not available at the same location.
Brain Writing is structured as follows:
1. Set out the theme together
2. Note individual solution idea(s) on a piece of paper or in an email
3. Pass on the solution ideas to the next person
   - in a room clockwise
   - in emails according to a pre-established order
4. Examine the idea of the person before you, build on it or develop a completely new idea
5. At the end of an agreed time the ideas are collected centrally
6. The result is presented and discussed
7. Select solution proposals afterwards

⇨ Tips
- Brain Writing often develops unusual and creative relationships between and combinations of ideas, including chains of ideas – at times this can exceed what brainstorming generates due to its more rigid structure and orientation.
- Brain Writing is especially suitable for heterogeneous teams with dominant and less dominant members. Persons with less dominant personalities are given more room to move and express their ideas.

DEFINE

Mind Mapping

🗀 Term / Description
Mind Mapping, creativity technique for structured idea collection and evaluation

MEASURE

🕐 When
In the Analyze and Design Phases, developing alternative concepts

◎ Goal
Support an extensive idea collection by visualizing connections between alternative solution ideas

▶▶ Steps
Mind Mapping is a technique for sketching semantic relationships between the ideas. Synergy effects are generated through the parallel utilization of language and images. A mind map revolving around the key theme emerges.

ANALYZE

Mind Map
Example: passenger seat

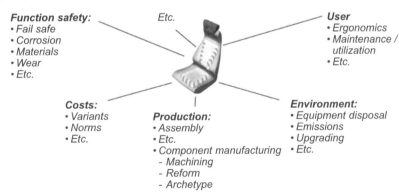

Function safety:
• *Fail safe*
• *Corrosion*
• *Materials*
• *Wear*
• *Etc.*

Etc.

User
• *Ergonomics*
• *Maintenance / utilization*
• *Etc.*

Costs:
• *Variants*
• *Norms*
• *Etc.*

Production:
• *Assembly*
• *Etc.*
• *Component manufacturing*
  - *Machining*
  - *Reform*
  - *Archetype*

Environment:
• *Equipment disposal*
• *Emissions*
• *Upgrading*
• *Etc.*

DESIGN

Depicting complex structures in a clear manner triggers further supportive or diversifying ideas. It also allows single aspects to be followed in detail.

VERIFY

SCAMPER

📁 **Term / Description**

SCAMPER, creativity technique for structured collection and evaluation of ideas

🕐 **When**

In the Analyze and Design Phases, developing alternative concepts

◎ **Goal**

Supplement the developed concept ideas with structured scrutinizing of the concept environment

▶▶ **Steps**

Structured scrutinizing of the concept environment generates and channels creative ideas.
This analysis is undertaken with a SCAMPER checklist.

SCAMPER Checklist

*S*ubstitute	• Which concept elements are replaceable and by what? • Are there comparable concepts from other companies, areas, etc.?
*C*ombine	• What can be combined in the concept? • Can this be combined with other ideas, broken down into modules and / or translated into a different illustration?
*A*dapt	• How can concept elements be adapted? • Are there parallels?
*M*odify	• How can concept elements be changed, enlarged or scaled down, strengths, dimensions and / or distances etc. be changed?
*P*ut to other uses	• How can concept elements be alienated from their designated function? • Can they be put to other uses?
*E*liminate / erase	• How can concept elements be eliminated or erased?
*R*everse / rearrange	• Which effects does a reversal of the concept elements have? • Can the order be rearranged? • Can the elements be substituted?

Morphological Box

📁 **Term / Description**

Morphological Box

🕐 **When**

In the Analyze and Design Phases, developing alternative concepts

◎ **Goal**

Develop alternative concept ideas

▶▶ **Steps**

In the framework of concept development the morphological box brings together all the conceivable combination possibilities of system features and their characteristics. This takes place on the basis of the defined and prioritized system functions.

Features are assigned to the prioritized functions. They are to be independent of one another where possible ("decoupled"). Relevant characteristics are now defined for each feature.

Morphological Box

Example: passenger seat

Characteristic (factor)	Feature (factor level)			
	1	*2*	*3*	*4*
Frame	Aluminum	Carbon	Steel	Wood
Cushioning	Velour	Imitate leather	Synthetic fiber	Polyester
Absorption	1 Spring element	2 Spring element	3 Spring element	4 Spring element
Floor attachment	Adjustment discs	Floor track	Combination disc / track	

Arrows in the matrix visualize every combination of the single feature characteristics that is promising economically and technologically.

DEFINE

MEASURE

ANALYZE

DESIGN

VERIFY

⇢ **Tips**

- For reasons of complexity no more than six features should be defined. If there is a high number of variations these should be distributed across detail matrixes.
- No features or their characteristics are to be evaluated or rejected beforehand. Even a solution that is as such suboptimal can represent a very good basis for optimal concepts when combined with others.
- The morphological box can in certain contexts highlight weak points in present solutions.
- The next step is to identify the optimal concept or enhance it further with the aid of the Pugh Matrix.

Benchmarking

📁 **Term / Description**

Benchmarking, system, product, process comparison, targeted internal and external comparison of performance

🕐 **When**

In the Measure, Analyze, Design Phases, developing alternative concepts

◎ **Goal**

Develop concept ideas using already existing systems

▸▸ **Steps**

Benchmarking compares one's own system with one (or more) other systems regarded as exemplary. This allows strengths and weaknesses to be identified and enables us to derive relevant hints at the current positioning of the product or process vis-à-vis competitors. A distinction is drawn between performance and process benchmarking.

Performance and Process Benchmarking

	Measure Phase	*Analyze Phase*	*Design Phase*
Performance- benchmarking	• Comparison with competitors from the customer viewpoint	• Best practice	• Best practice
Process- benchmarking	• Technological benchmarking	• General product and service pro- ducts • Function elements	• Alternatives for detailed design

Each benchmarking is carried out in three phases.

153

DEFINE

MEASURE

ANALYZE

DESIGN

VERIFY

Benchmarking Phases

1. Planning	2. Execution	3. Analysis
• Determine the scope of the benchmarking	• Prepare data collection plan	• Interpret data
• Identify benchmarking partner(s)	• Carry out data collection	• Derive concept ideas
• Determine relevant information		

The level of competition is considered when selecting suitable benchmarking systems.

Level of competition as criterion for selecting a comparative system for benchmarking

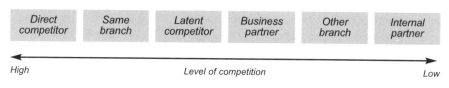

| Direct competitor | Same branch | Latent competitor | Business partner | Other branch | Internal partner |

High   *Level of competition*   Low

The higher the level of competition, the greater the effort needed for benchmarking or the more difficult benchmarking becomes.
It is therefore recommended to search for suitable internal benchmarking partners in one's own company. Suitable for comparison are internal processes, methods or company departments.

⇨ **Tips**

- Internal benchmarking demands willingness to be transparent and an open error management culture.
- In external benchmarking attention is to be especially paid to the comparability of data and key performance indicators. Companies often define these differently. This is to be considered when preparing and executing data collection and must be included in operational definitions.

Selecting the Best Concept

🗀 Term / Description
Selecting the best concept for fulfilling internal and external customer requirements

🕑 When
In the Analyze and Design Phases, selecting concept ideas

◎ Goal
Select the best design concept on the basis of the elaborated alternative concept ideas, taking into consideration the defined customer requirements

▶▶ Steps
The following evaluation procedure is suitable for selecting the best design concept:
- The selection procedure according to Pugh (Pugh Matrix)
- A comparison of elaborated concept ideas with management requirements (Critical to Business, CTBs)
- A statistical evaluation of the concept ideas using a Conjoint Analysis

DEFINE

MEASURE

ANALYZE

DESIGN

VERIFY

Selection Procedure Based on Pugh (Pugh Matrix)

▢ **Term / Description**

Pugh Analysis*, Pugh Matrix, selection procedure based on Pugh

◔ **When**

In the Analyze and Design Phases, selecting concept ideas

◎ **Goal**

Identify the best design concept through direct comparison and the sensible combination of specific feature characteristics for further optimization

▶▶ **Steps**

The Pugh Matrix can help identify the concept that best fulfills customer requirements. An analysis of strengths and weaknesses reveals those optimization approaches which enable a weak characteristic to be enhanced by a stronger one taken from another concept idea.

Criteria of efficiency (Critical to Business – CTBs) and effectiveness (Critical to Quality – CTQs) serve as the basis for evaluation. The criteria are weighed according to the priorities elaborated in the Measure Phase.

In the form of a matrix (Pugh) the alternative concept ideas are compared with an already existing or at least thoroughly analyzed standard concept.

A Pugh Matrix is presented on the following page.

* *Stuart Pugh (1991): Total Design - Integrated Methods for Successful Product Engineering, Pearson Education, Peachpit Press, Berkeley, CA, USA.*

Pugh Matrix
Comparison of alternative concept ideas

Alternative / Criteria	Concept 1	Concept 2 (Standard)	Concept 3	Prioritization
Criterion 1	+	0	-	3
Criterion 2	+	0	-	4
Criterion 3	0	0	+	2
Criterion 4	-	0	0	1
Aggregate +				
Aggregate -				
Aggregate 0				
Weighed aggregate +				
Weighed aggregate -				

A concept (usually the existing one or that of a competitor) is set as the standard and every criterion is given the value 0.

The alternative concept ideas are compared with this standard with respect to fulfilling the individual criteria. A better evaluation vis-à-vis the standard concept is tagged with a plus sign (+) and a poorer one with minus (-). For each concept the number of same valuations is added together and weighed according to the prioritization of the evaluated criteria (e.g. concept 1: prioritization of criterion 1 (=3) + prioritization of criterion 2 (=4) corresponds to the weighed aggregate + (=7)).

DEFINE

MEASURE

ANALYZE

DESIGN

VERIFY

157

Pugh Matrix
Valuation of alternative concept ideas

Alternative Criteria	Concept 1	Concept 2 (Standard)	Concept 3	Prioritization
Criterion 1	+	0	-	3
Criterion 2	+	0	-	4
Criterion 3	0	0	+	2
Criterion 4	-	0	0	1
Aggregate +	2	0	1	
Aggregate -	1	0	2	
Aggregate 0	1	4	1	
Weighed aggregate +	7	0	2	
Weighed aggregate -	1	0	7	

An analysis of the strengths and weaknesses of the alternative concept ideas is now possible by considering the following questions:
– Is there one concept that dominates the others?
– Why is it dominant?
– What are its weaknesses?
– Can these weaknesses be compensated by characteristics taken from other concept ideas (optimizing combination)?

A new solution approach can be developed out of this analysis: a good but still in part weak concept can be combined with the strengths of other concepts to generate an optimal solution.

Pugh Matrix
Optimizing weak characteristics of a best concept

Alternative \ Criteria	Concept 1	Concept 2 (Standard)	Concept 3	Prioritization
Criterion 1	+	0	-	3
Criterion 2	+	0	-	4
Criterion 3	0	0	+	2
Criterion 4	-	0	0	1
Aggregate +	2	0	1	
Aggregate -	1	0	2	
Aggregate 0	1	4	1	
Weighed aggregate +	7	0	2	
Weighed aggregate -	1	0	7	

Following an iterative procedure the optimized concept is continually compared and evaluated with the standard.

⇒ **Tips**
- A column-oriented focus on the dominating, best concept within the Pugh Matrix reveals possible conflicts / contradictions in the degree of fulfillment of single criteria.
- These contradictions can be described and solved with help of TRIZ methods.

DEFINE

MEASURE

ANALYZE

DESIGN

VERIFY

DEFINE

MEASURE

ANALYZE

DESIGN

VERIFY

Conjoint Analysis

☐ *Term/Description*
Conjoint Measurement, Trade-off Analysis, Conjoint Analysis, Decompositional Procedure

☾ When
In the Analyze and Design Phases, selecting concept ideas

◎ Goals
- Statistical evaluation of preferences and settings
- Identify the contribution of individual system features to the total benefit of a system (decompositional procedure)

▶▶ Steps
The Conjoint Analysis supports the analysis of customer preferences with respect to the characteristics of a system's features and attributes.

One way to evaluate preferences is direct surveying and gathering individual judgments. These enable the derivation or "composition" of an overall judgment on the system.

The Conjoint Analysis takes a multi-attribute or decompositional approach, i.e. the overall judgments (overall benefit) of relevant systems are decomposed into single judgments (part worth) with respect to the attributes and their characteristics.

Each system represents a conjoint of variable attributes. The contribution these attributes have for the overall benefit depends on their respective characteristics.

It is therefore possible to make relevant statements about the part worth of its attributes and their characteristics (X) on the basis of the user value.

DEFINE

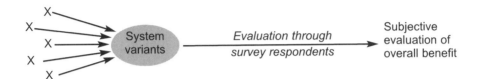

MEASURE

Conjoint Analysis and its Relationships

The data basis for a Conjoint Analysis consists of system variants or different solution approaches. A Conjoint Analysis is carried out as follows:

1. **Select attributes and their characteristics**

   The following aspects should be considered when selecting attributes and their characteristics:

   The attributes must be relevant, i.e. influence the buying decision.
   - The producer must be able to influence the attributes.
   - The attributes should be independent of one another.
   - Characteristics which are "musts" (exclusion criteria) are not to be utilized.
   - It must be feasible to realize these characteristics.
   - The individual characteristics must compensate one another (e.g. reducing the calorie content can be compensated by improving taste).
   - The number of attributes must be limited   the effort and expense of surveying grows exponentially.

ANALYZE

2. **Determine the survey design**

   Fictitious systems (so-called stimuli) are formed out of the different attribute characteristics. They are listed in a chart.

DESIGN

An example of Survey Design is presented on the following page.

VERIFY

DEFINE

MEASURE

ANALYZE

DESIGN

VERIFY

Survey Design

Stimuli no.	Installing	Cushioning	Cover	Seating comfort
1	Simple (< 1 min)	Firm	Fabric / leather	Armrest
2	Complicated (> 5 min)	Firm	Fabric / leather	No armrest
3	Simple (< 1 min)	Soft	Fabric / leather	No armrest
4	Complicated (> 5 min)	Soft	Fabric / leather	Armrest
5	Simple (< 1 min)	Firm	Synthetic	No armrest
6	Complicated (> 5 min)	Firm	Synthetic	Armrest
7	Simple (< 1 min)	Soft	Synthetic	Armrest
8	Complicated (> 5 min)	Soft	Synthetic	No armrest

Example: passenger seat

3. Collect data

The possible stimuli can be presented to the customer verbally, as a realized system, or in a computer animation. Various possibilities for evaluating are available:

– Ranking
– Evaluation using an ordinal scale or AHP (Analytic Hierarchy Process)
– One (or more) customer(s) is (are) asked to evaluate the fictitious systems (stimuli).

4. Estimate the benefit values

The connection between the identified preferences and the part worth

$$y_k = \sum_{j=1}^{J} \sum_{m=1}^{M_j} \beta_{jm} \cdot x_{jm} = \beta_{11} \cdot x_{11} + \beta_{12} \cdot x_{12} + \ldots + \beta_{JM_j} \cdot x_{JM_j}$$

of individual characteristics can be formulated as follows:
The valuation of the stimulus k matches its overall benefit y
y_k : overall benefit value for stimulus k.
The overall benefit is made up of the aggregate of all part worth.

The benefit value for a user – β – of an individual attribute j depends on its special characteristic m:

β_{jm} : part worth value for the characteristic m of attribute j.
Possible attribute characteristics which do not possess the evaluated stimuli k are removed from the calculation by the binary variable x:
x_{jm} : binary variable with the value 1 for existing attribute characteristics and the value 0 for non-existing attribute characteristics.

The mathematical specification of the overall benefit can also be achieved through an algorithm for Design of Experiments, e.g. with the help of Minitab®.

Conjoint Analysis with Minitab®

▶▶ *Steps*

A Conjoint Analysis using the software program Minitab® (Factorial Design) derives the optimal combination of possible attribute characteristics from the identified overall benefit of the individual stimuli and thus shows which fictitious system (stimuli) has the highest overall user value for the customer. The team wishes to locate those characteristics with which a passenger seat can best be marketed and fits the needs of the target customer.

The four selected key attributes and their characteristics are:
1. Installing the seat: simple (< 1 min) vs. complicated (> 5 min)
2. Cushioning: firm vs. soft
3. Cover: fabric / leather vs. synthetic
4. Seating comfort: armrest vs. no armrest

Because the number of possible stimuli rises exponentially with the number of variable attributes, it often makes sense to use a reduced experiment design. Such a fractional factorial or part factorial design can be drawn up in Minitab®.

DEFINE

MEASURE

ANALYZE

DESIGN

VERIFY

A Conjoint Analysis with Minitab® is presented on the following page.
Conjoint Analysis with Minitab®

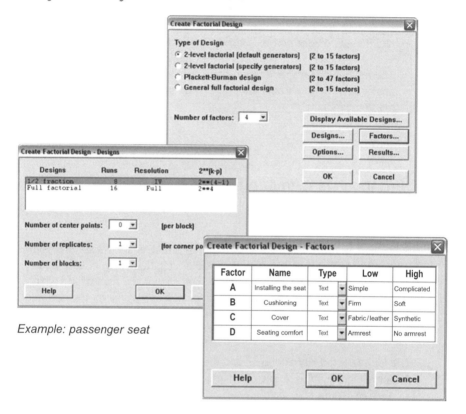

Example: passenger seat

The number of observed attributes (number of factors) and their characteristics (factor levels) are entered into Minitab®.

The fictitious systems can be evaluated in a pairwise comparison using an AHP or sorting it into a ranked scale.

The derived priority is captured as the overall benefit value in Minitab®.

The scaling of the overall benefit value ranges from 1 (worst) to 8 (best).

Minitab® Worksheet for Conjoint Analysis

↓	C1	C2	C3	C4	C5-T	C6-T	C7-T	C8-T	C9
	StdOrder	RunOrder	CenterPT	Blocks	Installing	Cushioning	Cover	Seating comfort	Ranking
1	1	1	1	1	Simple (< 1 min)	Firm	Fabric/leather	Armrest	6
2	2	2	1	1	Complicated (> 5 min)	Firm	Fabric/leather	No armrest	4
3	3	3	1	1	Simple (< 1 min)	Soft	Fabric/leather	No armrest	8
4	4	4	1	1	Complicated (> 5 min)	Soft	Fabric/leather	Armrest	7
5	5	5	1	1	Simple (< 1 min)	Firm	Synthetic	No armrest	1
6	6	6	1	1	Complicated (> 5 min)	Firm	Synthetic	Armrest	3
7	7	7	1	1	Simple (< 1 min)	Soft	Synthetic	Armrest	5
8	8	8	1	1	Complicated (> 5 min)	Soft	Synthetic	No armrest	2

Example: passenger seat
> The first graph for analyzing data is generated.

Minitab® Pareto Chart from DOE

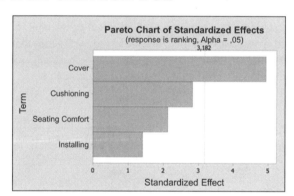

Example: passenger seat

> In this case the Pareto Chart shows that the seat cover is the most important attribute. The other attributes do not appear to be statistically significant.
> A Main Effects Plot can then reveal which characteristics are preferred.

165

DEFINE

MEASURE

ANALYZE

DESIGN

VERIFY

DEFINE

MEASURE

ANALYZE

DESIGN

VERIFY

A Minitab® Main Effects Plot from DOE is presented on the following page.

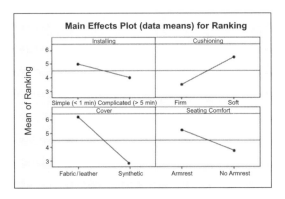

Minitab® Main Effects Plot from DOE
Example: passenger seat

Here it is clear that a simple installation, a soft cushioning, a fabric/leather cover, and a seat with armrests are preferred by the target customers.

The result in the Minitab® session window confirms this.

Estimated Effects and Coefficients for Ranking (coded units)

Term	Effect	CoefSE	Coef	T	P	≤ 0.05
Constant		4.500	0.3536	12.73	0.001	
Installing	-1.000	-0.500	0.3536	-1.41	0.252	
Cushioning	2.000	1.000	0.3536	2.83	0.066	
Cover	-3.500	-1.750	0.3536	-4.95	0.016	
Seating						
Comfort	-1.500	-0.750	0.3536	-2.12	0.124	

S = 1   R-Sq = 92.86%   R-Sq(adj) = 83.33%

Analysis of Variance for Ranking (coded units)

Source	DF	Seq SS	Adj SS	Adj MS	F	P
Main Effects	4	39.000	39.000	9.750	9.75	0.046
Residual Error	3	3.000	3.000	1.000		
Total	7	42.000				

DEFINE

Minitab® Session Window from DOE
Example: passenger seat

The p-values indicate which attributes are statistically significant. Only the value generated for the cover lies beneath the significance level of 0.05.

By maximizing ranking the Minitab® "Response Optimizer" indicates the attribute characteristics which the system with the highest overall benefit should have for the customer.

MEASURE

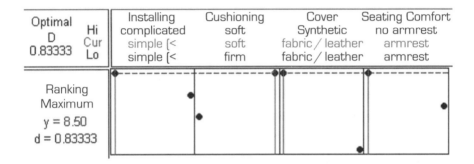

Optimal D 0.83333	Hi Cur Lo	Installing complicated simple [< simple [<	Cushioning soft soft firm	Cover Synthetic fabric / leather fabric / leather	Seating Comfort no armrest armrest armrest
Ranking Maximum y = 8.50 d = 0.83333					

ANALYZE

Minitab® Response Optimizer from DOE
Example: passenger seat

Result of the Conjoint Analysis:
The optimal overall benefit value of y = 8.5 is achieved by a seat that is simple to install, has a soft cushioning with a fabric/leather cover and armrests. The optimal overall benefit value exceeds in this case even the highest ranking/the highest overall benefit of the evaluated stimuli.

DESIGN

VERIFY

Optimizing Design Concept

📁 **Term / Description**

Optimize Design Concept

🕙 **When**

In the Analyze and Design Phases

◎ **Goals**

– Eliminate potential occurring contradictions in the selected concept
– Derive the necessary requirements to necessary resources

▶▶ **Steps**

The contradictions identified in the correlation roof of the House of Quality (Measure Phase) and in the Pugh Matrix (selecting the concept in the Analyze Phase) can now be resolved with the help of TRIZ methods.

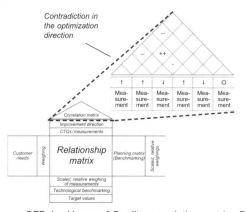

QFD 1 – House of Quality: correlation matrix   Pugh Matrix: analyzing the concepts

Resources are required to further develop an optimal concept that is free of contradictions. The requirements to these resources are identified and described. A basis for decisions on releasing and clearing the necessary resources is to be formulated.

TRIZ –

Resolving Conflicts in the Selected Concept

📁 **Term / Description**
TRIZ*, TIPS (Theory of Inventive Problem Solving)

🕙 **When**
In the Analyze and Design Phases, optimizing the design concept

◎ **Goal**
Innovatively eliminate contradictions in the selected concept without compromising quality

▶▶ **Steps**
TRIZ offers a series of methods and tools capable of resolving a variety of problems which crop up when developing a concept. These methods are basically oriented towards elevating the concrete problem onto an abstract level, a step that allows an abstract solution to be found based on general principles. This is then converted into a specific solution by creativity, expertise and experience.

TRIZ – the Principal Approach

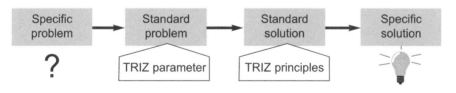

Every possible problem belongs to one of the following five main groups; the various tools and methods of TRIZ provide solutions.

---

* *Altshuller, Genrich S. (10.15.1926-9.24.1998)*

DEFINE

MEASURE

ANALYZE

DESIGN

VERIFY

DEFINE

MEASURE

ANALYZE

DESIGN

VERIFY

Main Groups in TRIZ

Engineering/ technical conflict	Physical conflicts	Incomplete functional structures	Escalating complexity	System optimization
Improving the operation of one object leads to a deterioration of another operation	Useful and harmful actions impact on the same object	There are insufficient useful functions or the required useful functions are missing	The system is too complex and expensive	Although the current system improvement is necessary to attain competitive advantage

⇨ **Tips**

- A contradiction or conflict exists whenever the level of fulfillment for one requirement rises, and the level of a different requirement is reduced as a result.
- Technical and physical contradictions are often due to the same single conflict.

Engineering Contradictions

📁 Term / Description
Engineering Contradictions, Technical Contradictions

🕐 When
In the Analyze and Design Phases, optimizing the design concept

◎ Goal
Innovative elimination of engineering contradictions – without trade-offs – in the selected concept by transferring the problem to 39 technical parameters and applying 40 innovative principles.

▶▶ Steps
An engineering or technical contradiction exists in a system when improving one parameter results in the deterioration of another.

Engineering Contradiction
Example: engine

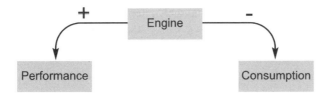

The TRIZ method sets out 39 general engineering parameters which may contradict one another.

The 39 engineering parameters set out in TRIZ are presented on the following page.

DEFINE

MEASURE

ANALYZE

DESIGN

VERIFY

171

DEFINE

MEASURE

ANALYZE

DESIGN

VERIFY

The 39 Engineering Parameters in TRIZ

1. Weight of a moving object	15. Durability of a moving object	29. Production precision
2. Weight of a stationary object	16. Durability of a stationary object	30. External effects harming an object
3. Length of a moving object	17. Temperature	31. Harmful factors generated by the objectmovingmoving
4. Length of a stationary object	18. Illumination intensity	
5. Area of a moving object	19. Energy use by a moving object	32. Ease of production
6. Area of a stationary object	20. Energy use by a stationary object	33. Ease of operation
7. Volume of a moving object	21. Power	34. Ease of repair
8. Volume of a stationary object	22. Loss of energy	35. Adaptability or versatility
9. Speed	23. Loss of substance	36. Complexity in structure
10. Force	24. Loss of information	37. Complexity in measuring and monitoring
11. Stress or pressure	25. Loss of time	
12. Shape	26. Quantity of substance / matter	38. Extent of automation
13. Stability of an object's composition	27. Reliability	39. Productivity
14. Strength	28. Measurement accuracy	

The defined engineering parameters are divided into physical-technical factors (e.g. weight, length, volume) and system-technical factors (e.g. reliability, productivity).

The 39 engineering parameters in overview:

1. *Weight of a moving object*
   The effects generated by a moving object's own weight on an area (leading element). Objects are moving when they can change their position on their own or through external forces.

2. *Weight of a stationary object*
   The effects generated by a stationary object's own weight on an area (fundament). Objects are stationary when they cannot change their position on their own or through external forces.

3. *Length of a moving object*
   Dimensions – length, breadth, height or depth of a moving object.

4. *Length of a stationary object*
   Dimensions – length, breadth, height or depth of a stationary object.

5. *Area of a moving object*
   Area of an object that can change its position in space through the effect of internal or external force.

6. *Area of a stationary object*
   Area of an object that cannot change its position in space through the effect of internal or external force.

7. *Volume of a moving object*
   Volume of an object that can change its position in space through the effect of internal or external force.

8. *Volume of a stationary object*
   Volume of an object that cannot change its position in space through the effect of internal or external force.

9. *Speed*
   Working or process speed with which an operation or a process can be executed.

10. *Force, intensity*
    Force to effect physical changes on an object or system.
    These changes can be whole or partial, permanent or temporary.

11. *Stress or pressure*
    Amount of force that generates stress or pressure within the impact sphere of an object.

12. *Shape*
    Shape of an object or system. The shape can change entirely or partially, permanently or temporarily while force impacts on it.

13. *Stability of an object's composition*
    Stability of the system during internal or external effects on its parts or subsystems.

14. *Strength*
    Limit defined by surrounding conditions within which no material malfunction is allowed to take place due to external infringement of the object or system.

15. *Durability of a moving object*
    Duration or time span in which a moving object can fully fulfill its function.

173

16. *Durability of a stationary object*
Duration or time span in which a stationary object can fully fulfill its function.

17. *Temperature*
Temperature rise or fall of an object or a system while fulfilling its function.

18. *Illumination intensity*
Intensity of light in, around or through the system, including the light quality and other characteristics of light.

19. *Energy use by a moving object*
Energy needed by a stationary object or system.

20. *Energy use by a stationary object*
Energy needed by a stationary object or system.

21. *Power*
Power (work/unit of time) that is necessary to actually perform a function.

22. *Loss of energy*
Increased incapacity of an object or system to incorporate energy, especially when production is not taking place.

23. *Loss of substance*
Reduction or loss of substance of an object or system, especially when production is not taking place.

24. *Loss of information*
Reduction or loss of data or the input of a system.

25. *Loss of time*
Necessary increase of time to carry out an operation.

26. *Quantity of substance/matter*
Number or quantity of elements comprising an object or system.

27. *Reliability*
The capacity of an object or system to fulfill its function over a specific time span or cycle.

DEFINE

28. *Measurement accuracy*
    The accuracy of a measurement in relation to the real value.

29. *Production precision*
    The precision of production in relation to the construction specifications.

30. *External effects harming the object*
    External factors which reduce the efficiency or quality of the object or system.

MEASURE

31. *Harmful factors generated by the object*
    Internal factors which reduce the efficiency or quality of the object or system.

32. *Ease of production*
    Objects or systems can be produced easily.

33. *Ease of operation*
    Objects or systems can be easily operated.

34. *Ease of repair*
    Objects or systems can be easily repaired after intensive use or damage.

ANALYZE

35. *Adaptability or versatility*
    The capacity of an object or system to adapt to changed conditions.

36. *Complexity in structure*
    Number and diversity of elements comprising individual objects or systems as well as their interactions.

37. *Complexity in measuring and monitoring*
    Number and diversity of elements to measure and monitor objects and systems as well as the costs for an acceptable error contribution.

DESIGN

38. *Extent of automation*
    The possibilities to operate objects or systems without the aid of people.

39. *Productivity*
    The relationship between operating time and total time.

VERIFY

DEFINE

MEASURE

ANALYZE

DESIGN

VERIFY

The paired comparison of technical parameters in matrix form facilitates their application and supports both the transference of the concrete conflict as well as deriving the relevant innovative principles. This matrix is known as the "contradiction matrix".

Within the frame of TRIZ, 40 innovative principles are formulated as generally applicable solution approaches for conflicts defined via the technical parameters.

The 40 Innovative Principles of TRIZ

1. Segmentation	15. Dynamics	27. Cheap short-living objects
2. Taking out	16. Partial or excessive actions ("less is more")	28. Mechanics substitution
3. Local quality		29. Pneumatics and hydraulics
4. Asymmetry	17. Another dimension	30. Flexible shells and thin films
5. Merging	18. Mechanical vibration	31. Porous materials
6. Universality	19. Periodic action	32. Color changes
7. Nested doll	20. Continuity of useful action	33. Homogeneity
8. Anti-weight	21. Skipping	34. Discarding and recovering
9. Preliminary anti-action	22. "Blessing in disguise" or "Turn lemons into lemonade"	35. Parameter changes
10. Preliminary action		36. Phase transitions
11. Preventive activities / cushioning	23. Feedback	37. Thermal expansion
12. Equipotentiality	24. "Intermediary"	38. Strong oxidants
13. The other way around / Inversion	25. Self-service	39. Inert atmosphere
14. Spheroidality – Curvature	26. Copying	40. Composite materials

The 40 innovative principles in an overview:

1. *Segmentation*
   a. Divide an object into independent part-objects, e.g.:
      – Build a PC out of modular components
      – Replace a large truck by a truck with trailer
   b. Simplify the decomposition / assembly of an object, e.g.:
      – Module system
      – Quick locks with tubes
   c. Increase the degree segmentation of an object, e.g.:
      – Freely extendable garden hose

2. *Taking out*
   a. Eliminate interfering functions, components, or qualities of an object, e.g.:

    – Relocate a noisy compressor outside the work area or building

    – Relocate loud units of air-conditioning system outside the living area

  b. Single out and restrict to necessary elements or functions of objects,e.g.:

    – Recording and playing barking dogs as part of a security alarm

    – Playing animal noises to frighten off birds at airports

3. *Local quality*

  a. Change the uniform (constant) structure of an object or its environment to a non-uniform structure, e.g.:

    – To combat coal dust in a mine a fine spray of water is spread across the working area; however, this hampers work in the drill zone

    – The working areas in the mine are separated by a further layer of water, this time larger drops, which limit the fine spray locally

  b. Distribute the different functions of an object among different elements, e.g.:

    – Pencil with eraser

    – Swiss army knife

  c. Create optimal conditions for each sub-function of an object, e.g.:

    – Lunchbox with special compartments for hot and cold beverages and food

4. *Asymmetry*

  a. Replace symmetrical shapes and forms by asymmetrical ones, e.g.:

    – Asymmetrical vessels or asymmetrical mixing forms improve the mixing of materials (blenders, cement mixers)

    – Reinforce the exterior of tyres to minimize the harmful impact of curbs

  b. Increase existing asymmetrical effects

5. *Merging*

  a. Concentration of identical or similar objects and operations in the same room, e.g.:

    – Merge PCs into a network

    – Electronic chips on both sides of a plug-in card

  b. Operations carried out simultaneously or promptly (bringing them together in time), e.g.:

    – Medical diagnostic instrument analyzing different parameters of blood simultaneously

    – Lawnmower fitted with mulch cover

6. *Universality*

Multifunctional design of objects reduces the quantity of other parts, e.g.:
   – Sofa that can be converted into a bed
   – A stroller that can be converted into a car safety seat
   – Minivan seats which can be used to sit, sleep, or transport goods

7. *Nested Doll (Matryoshka)*
   a. Space-saving placement of identical objects into one another, e.g.:
      – Matryoshka, Russian nested doll
      – Stackable seats to save space when storing
      – Telescopic antenna
      – Refillable drop-action pencil
      – Camera lens with zoom function
   b. Space-saving placement of different objects into each other, e.g.:
      – Storage function of automatic seatbelts
      – Extendable aircraft landing gear

8. *Anti-weight*
   a. Reduce the weight of an object by generating buoyant force, e.g.:
      – Air tanks in the hull of a ship or in a submarine
      – Sandwich construction in planes, surfboards, etc.
   b. Utilize dynamic forces, e.g.:
      – Wing shape of aircraft creates lift
      – Traction for sports cars through rear wing

9. *Preliminary anti-action*
   a. Take steps to counter or control harmful effects or undesirable stress, e.g.:
      – Spoke of a wheel
      – Bolted connection to absorb force

10. *Preliminary action*
   a. Take into account predictable actions early, e.g.:
      – Craft knife with blade segments which can be broken off
      – Tool change system
   b. Spatially sensible arrangement of necessary objects which are required in due course, e.g.:
      – Replenishment pull system in production

DEFINE

11. Preventive activities / cushioning

Take into account the possible consequences of an object with relatively low reliability by counter activities, e.g.:

- Back-up parachute
- Magnetized anti-theft strip on consumer goods

12. Equipotentiality

Create a spatially constant level, e.g.:

- Canal locks for regulating the level of water and / or elevating or lowering ships
- Work on the underbody or engine (from below) of a car

MEASURE

13. The other way around / Inversion

  a. Invert the actions used to solve a problem, e.g.:
    "Bring the mountain to Mohammed"
  b. Invert the moving and non-moving qualities, e.g.:
    - Rotate the part instead of the tool
    - Ergometer, treadmill
  c. Reverse the object or process
    - Empty the contents of rotating containers (rail, ship)

ANALYZE

14. Spheroidality – Curvature (in all dimensions)

  a. Curvature of straight lines and flat surfaces, e.g.:
    - Parabolic mirror
  b. Extend two-dimensional movements, e.g.:
    - Computer mouse
    - Trackball
    - Ballpoint pen
  c. Use centrifugal forces, e.g.:
    - Centrifugal casting
    - Clothes dryer

DESIGN

15. Dynamics

  a. Variable design of an object or its environment, e.g.:
    - Automatically adjustable car seat, rearview mirror, steering wheel
  b. Divide an object into parts or segments which move relatively to one another, e.g.:
    - "Gooseneck" for car radios, flashlights, lamps
    - Clockworks
    - Gears
  c. Turn fixed objects or rigid processes into movable or replaceable ones

VERIFY

16. *Partial or excessive actions ("less is more")*
    a. Extend or limit individual object functions, e.g.:
       – Rotate freshly painted cylinder to remove excess paint

17. *Another dimension*
    a. Avoid obstacles by adding further dimensions, e.g.:
       – Move an infrared computer mouse in the room instead of across a surface
       – 3D chess
    b. Utilize storage possibilities, e.g.:
       – CD jukebox
       – Tool changing systems
    c. Change of position, e.g.:
       – Dump truck
    d. Project objects into neighboring areas, e.g.:
       – Concave reflector on the north side to illuminate a glasshouse

18. *Mechanical vibration*
    a. Utilize the vibrations made by objects, e.g.:
       – Vibrating knife to remove a plaster cast as a way of preventing damage to the surface
       – Vibration of funnels to optimize the flow of abrasives
    b. Increase the frequency of vibrating objects
    c. Exploit an object's own resonant frequency
    d. Transition from mechanical to piezo-electric vibrators, e.g.:
       – Cleaning of lab equipment in ultrasonic bath
    e. Functional combination of ultrasonic vibrations with electromagnetic fields

19. *Periodic action*
    a. Transition from continuous to periodic actions, e.g.:
       – Flashing of warning lights to improve visibility
       – Uncouple rusted screws with impulses instead of continuous exertion of force
    b. Change the frequency of periodic actions
    c. Use recurrent pauses, e.g.:
       – Additionally achieved actions

20. *Continuity of useful action*
    – All components work continuously at full load
    – Eliminate all idle times or intermittent actions

21. *Skipping*

Raise the speed of damaging or dangerous actions: work areas that are harmful but indispensable for the process have to be finished or exited as quickly as possible

22. *"Blessing in disguise", converting harmful factors into positive effects*
    a. Positive use of harmful factors or effects – especially from the environment
    b. Eliminate harmful factors by combining them with one another
    c. Eliminate a harmful factor by amplifying it

23. *Feedback*
    a. Introduce feedback
    b. Vary or reverse feedback

24. *Intermediary*
    a. Integrate a subobject to transfer an effect, e.g.:
       Cooled electrodes and another fluid metal with a fusion point lying between them to avoid energy loss when tension is applied to a fluid metal
    b. Temporarily connect an object with another, easily detachable object

25. *Self-service*
    a. Enable an object to serve itself in performing auxiliary functions,e.g.:
       Abrasive surface design of a bottling apparatus for abrasive materials to generate a continuous "healing of itself"
    b. Use waste resources or "byproduct analogy" (energy, materials)

26. *Copying*
    a. Replace complex, expensive, fragile objects or objects which are difficult to manage with cheap, simple copies
    b. Replace an object or process with optical copies, where needed with changed scales
    c. Replace optical copies with infrared or ultraviolet copies, e.g.:
       Measure high objects using their shadows

27. *Cheap short-living objects*

Replace a sophisticated, expensive object with a disposable, cheap object:
    – Disposable diapers
    – Single-use scalpels
    – Single-use syringes

28. *Mechanics substitution*
   a. Replace a mechanical system with an optical, acoustic or odorized system
   b. Use interactions of electrical, magnetic or electromagnetic fields with the object
   c. Move from static to movable fields, from constant to alterable, and from unstructured to structured fields
   d. Use ferromagnetic particles, e.g.:
      – Improve the connection between a metal and a thermoplastic by attaching an electromagnetic field to the metal

29. *Pneumatics and hydraulics*
   Use gas and liquid parts of an object instead of its massive parts. Apply parts that are inflatable or filled with liquids, an air cushion, or hydro-static and hydro-reactive parts. Package of fragile goods in padded envelopes or air cushions during transport

30. *Flexible shells and thin films*
   a. Deploy malleable, flexible shells and thin films
   b. Isolate an object from its environment using flexible shells and thin films, e.g.:
      – Spray leaves with a PE film to protect a plant from evaporation

31. *Porous materials*
   a. Porous design of an object or its elements (inserts, coatings, etc)
   b. Fill an already porous object

32. *Color changes*
   a. Change the color of an object or its external environment
   b. Change the transparency of an object or its external environment
   c. Make visible an object difficult to recognize by adding color
   d. Use fluorescent colors

33. *Homogeneity*
   Apply identical or very similar materials, e.g.:
   – Abrasive surface design of a bottling apparatus for abrasive materials to achieve a continuous "healing of itself"

34. *Discarding and recovering*
   a. Discard object parts which are no longer necessary or have fulfilled their function, e.g.:

    – Rocket or missile stages
    – Bullet casings
  b. Modify used parts during an operation
  c. Restore used parts during an operation

35. *Parameter changes*
Do not only make use of simple changes of an object's aggregate state (into gas, liquid, solid) but also transitions into "pseudo" or "quasi" states and interim states (elastic, solid bodies, thixotropy substances)

36. *Phase transitions*
Exploit the effects during a phase transition of a substance, e.g.:
  – Exploit evaporation energy of water
  – Fill hollow bodies with water in order to measure the expansion of the bodies or to split them once the water freezes

37. *Thermal expansion*
  a. Use changes in the volume of materials caused by warmth
  b. Combine materials with different thermal expansion, e.g.:
    Bimetals as switches

38. *Strong oxidants*
  a. Enrich air with oxygen
  b. Replace enriched air with pure oxygen
  c. Expose air or oxygen to ionizing radiation
  d. Deploy ozonized oxygen
  e. Replace ozonized (or ionized) oxygen with ozone

39. *Inert atmosphere*
  a. Replace the normal environment with an inert one
  b. Carry out the process in a vacuum, e.g.:
    Process groceries under protective atmosphere (e.g.: nitrogen)

40. *Composite materials*
Apply composite materials, e.g.: aircraft construction (carbon fiber composites)

TRIZ Contradiction Matrix

🗁 **Term / Description**
Contradiction Matrix

🕑 **When**
In the Analyze and Design Phases, optimizing the design concept

◎ **Goal**
Convert specific problems into technical parameters and derive relevant innovative principles for generating specific solutions

▸▸ **Steps**
The specific problem is formulated as a contradiction between two general technical parameters. It is advisable to persue the following strategy:
– Which technical parameter of the system is to be improved ("improving feature")?
– Which technical parameters does this desired improvement influence negatively ("worsening feature")?

The innovative principles suitable for solving the formulated contradiction can be gathered from the matrix based on the paired parameters.
From these innovative principles a specific solution is then derived for an innovative resolution of the contradiction without compromise, enabling the team to use its creativity, expertise and experience.

An application of the TRIZ contradiction matrix is presented on the following page.

DEFINE

Applying the TRIZ Contradiction Matrix

Formulate the specific technical contradictions ▶ Describe these as a general, technical contradiction ▶ Contradiction matrix ▶ General, potential solutions for the technical contradiction ▶ Generate a specific solution to resolve the technical contra-diction

39 technical parameters

40 innovative principles

Example TRIZ Contradiction Matrix

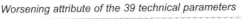
Worsening attribute of the 39 technical parameters

One of the 39 technical parameters to be improved or maintained

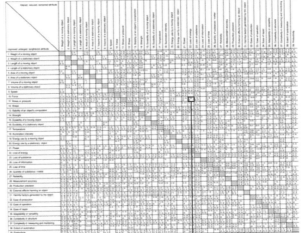

Suitable, general, potential solutions for the technical contradiction from the 40 innovative principles

An enlarged TRIZ contradiction matrix is presented in the appendix.

MEASURE

ANALYZE

⇨ **Tip**

The contradiction matrix reduces the effort needed to investigate possible innovative principles by providing a direct assignment according to the defined technical parameters. However, in case of doubt, each of the 40 innovative principles should be examined to see if they are applicable.

DESIGN

VERIFY

185

Applying a TRIZ contradiction matrix
Example: passenger seat

While developing the new passenger seat the team has identified a conflict between having "quick seat installation" and "theft-proof seats".
According to the TRIZ approach, this represents a general technical contradiction between the improving parameters:
- 16: Durability of a stationary object (theft-proof)
- 30: External factors (theft)

and the attributes worsening because of this:
- 25: Loss of time
- 34: Repair kindness

The contradiction matrix shows that the following parameter combinations can provide a solution for this conflict:
A: 16 to 25 → innovative principles: 28, 20, 10, 16
B: 16 to 34 → innovative principles: 1
C: 30 to 25 → innovative principles: 35, 18, 34
D: 30 to 34 → innovative principles: 35, 10, 2

The team persues the following interesting solution approaches:
- Innovative principle 2: "Separating and taking out – limiting objects to necessary elements or functions"
- Innovative principle 10: "Preliminary action – spatially sensible arrangement of required objects in due course"

Proceeding from the identified innovative principles the team elaborates a specific solution for overcoming the conflict between the CTQs "theft-proof" and "quick seat installation". This is done in a brainstorming session:
- A continuous holding rail separated from the seat construction in which all of the seats can be installed one behind the other
- This rail is fixed to the floor and its attachments can only be closed or opened from a central switch
- This reduces installation time while raising security against theft because the seat can no longer be disassembled with conventional tools

⇨ **Tips**
- The identified TRIZ innovative principles represent recommendations for changing the technical system – they are not to be taken literally. Fantasy and creativity are needed when developing specific solutions!
- Combinations and reversals (e.g. "merging" instead of "segmenting") of the proposed innovative principles can also lead to meaningful solutions.

DEFINE

MEASURE

ANALYZE

DESIGN

VERIFY

DEFINE

MEASURE

ANALYZE

DESIGN

VERIFY

Physical Contradictions

☐ **Term / Description**
Physical Contradictions

🕑 **When**
In the Analyze and Design Phases, optimizing the design concept

◎ **Goal**
Innovative elimination of physical contradictions in the selected concept without compromises

▶▶ **Steps**
A physical contradiction exists in a system when the whole system or one of its components has to take on two contradictory states to fulfill a parameter.

Physical Contradictions according to TRIZ
Example

Parameter xy

- sweet – sour
- open – closed
- short – long
- hot – cold
- gaseous – solid
- big – small
- inflammable – non-flammable

In principle there are three possibilities for solving physical contradictions:
- Separate the contradictory requirements
- Fulfill the contradictory requirements
- Avoid the contradiction

DEFINE

MEASURE

ANALYZE

DESIGN

VERIFY

Possible solutions for physical contradictions according to TRIZ

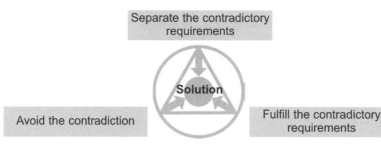

Separate the contradictory requirements

Solution

Avoid the contradiction

Fulfill the contradictory requirements

Examples

The production of machine parts from of a specific type of steel requires that the steel be heated to 1200°C before it can be formed. As it turns out, the surface of the material is damaged by the reaction with air when the temperature is heated above 800°C.

On the one hand the steel must have a temperature of 1200°C if it is to be moldable, while on the other it cannot become hotter than 800°C, otherwise damage occurs.

A firm produces oval glass elements with a thickness of 1 mm. In a first working step rectangular parts are cut and their edges grinded off. These parts break, however, due to the slight diameter. On the one hand the parts have to be thin in diameter to match customer requirements, but on the other hand they also have to be thick enough so they don't break when they are grinded.

Physical Contradictions according to TRIZ
Example

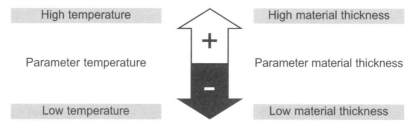

High temperature

Parameter temperature

Low temperature

High material thickness

Parameter material thickness

Low material thickness

189

Separating the Contradictory Requirements

Steps:
To decide how the contradictory attributes can be separated the problem has to be assigned to one of the following four categories:

A Separation in relation to location
B Separation in relation to time
C Separation in relationships
D Separation in relation to the system level

A ***Separation in relation to location***
The object's contradictory attributes shall be manifest at different places. These separate locations are known as operational zone 1 and operational zone 2.

Separation in relation to location

+ Operational zone 1   **−** Operational zone 2

Example:
The steel parts must be heated to 1200°C inwardly, but their surfaces are not to exceed 800°C.

Suitable innovative principles in this case are:
1. Segmentation and division
2. Taking out
3. Local quality
4. Asymmetry
7. Interlacing
17. Another dimension

DEFINE

B Separation in relation to time
The object's contradictory attributes shall be manifest at different times. These separate times are known as operational time 1 and operational time 2.

Separation in relation to location

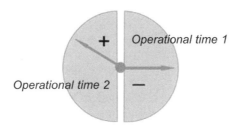

Operational time 1

Operational time 2

MEASURE

Example:
An umbrella must be as large as possible when it is raining. When it isn't raining the umbrella must be as compact as possible.

Suitable innovative principles in this case are:
9. Preliminary anti-action
10. Preliminary action
11. Beforehand cushioning
15. Dynamics
34. Discarding and recovering

ANALYZE

C Separation in the relationships
The object's contradictory attributes are required in relation to other objects.

Separation in the relationships

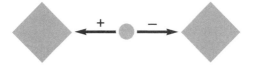

DESIGN

VERIFY

DEFINE

MEASURE

ANALYZE

DESIGN

VERIFY

Example:
With regard to gravitational force aircraft wings must be as small as possible; for propulsion and uplift they must be as large as possible.

Suitable innovative principles in this case are:
3. Local quality
17. Another dimension
19. Periodic action
31. Porous materials
35. Parameter changes
40. Composite materials

D   Separation in relation to the system levels
The object's contradictory attributes are required on different system levels.

Separation in relation to the system levels

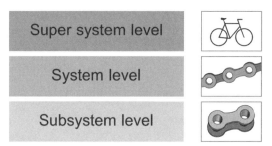

Super system level	
System level	
Subsystem level	

Example:
The system bicycle chain must be flexible on the super system level but stable and solid on the subsystem level.

Suitable innovative principles in this case are:
1. Segmentation and division
5. Merging
12. Equipotentiality
33. Homogeneity

Fulfilling the Contradictory Requirements

Steps:
So-called "smart materials" can fulfill contradictory requirements in some cases.

These include for example:
*   **Shape Memory Alloys (SMA):** these are metals which possess a "memory" and can take on different shapes when they are heated or cooled.
*   **Electrorheological or magnetorheological fluids:** these fluids change their viscosity within milliseconds (fluid - solid) when an electrical or magnetic field affects them. One example is how the fluid in a hydraulic cycle can take on the function of a medium for pressure transmission at the same time as it acts as a steering medium. Electorheological flow resistance allows valves to be developed which have no need for movable parts and so operate almost wear-free.

Avoiding the Contradiction

Steps:
New approaches can make resolving rigid conflicts superfluous.

Example:
When rain is accompanied by strong winds we need a large umbrella to keep us dry. On the other hand though, the umbrella must be very small in order not to offer the wind much contact surface. This contradiction becomes unimportant as soon as one uses a suitably designed raincoat which covers the whole body.

⇒ **Tip**

The existing system often forms the starting point for the problem definition and the direction selected is unconsciously very narrow in its dimensions, so that only improvement approches and no genuine solutions become visible for the fundamental problem. This can be prevented by "liberating" oneself from the known principle or solution and starting again from the "original state".

DEFINE

MEASURE

ANALYZE

DESIGN

VERIFY

DEFINE

MEASURE

ANALYZE

DESIGN

VERIFY

Sufield Analysis –
Incomplete Functional Structures

📁 **Term / Description**

Sufield Analysis, Substance-Field Analysis, Wepol Analysis

🕐 **When**

In the Analyze and Design Phases, optimizing the design concept

◎ **Goal**

Eliminate incomplete functional structures

▶▶ **Steps**

In the Sufield Analysis a technical system is defined as the combination of at least two substances (S1 and S2) which interact with the aid of a field (F). Every system can be depicted in this way.

Sufield Analysis

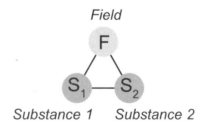

Field

Substance 1   Substance 2

S_1 is the substance that is to be changed, processed, transformed and / or controlled.
The substance S_2 serves as the tool, instrument, or medium.
The field F represents the force or energy with which S_2 affects S_1.

Sufield Analysis
Example

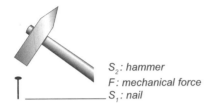

S_2: hammer
F: mechanical force
S_1: nail

A Sufield model abstracts a real problem and solves it with the help of general principles.

Steps for a Sufield Analysis

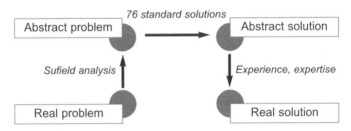

The Sufield analysis distinguishes between four basic models of technical systems:
1. Complete systems
2. Incomplete systems
3. Complete but inefficient systems
4. Complete but harmful systems

The basic model is visualized with a defined symbolism.

195

Symbols for the Sufield Analysis

$\triangle$	Symbolic form of a Sufield model
——————	Unspecific effect
————▶	Desired (specific) effect
◀————▶	Interaction
- - - - ▶	Insufficient effect
∿∿↗	Harmful effect
⇨	Indicates the direction from given to desired Sufield model
F ————▶	Field affects a substance
————▶ F	Field generated by a substance
F'	Modified field
S'	Modified substance

1. **Complete system**

   A complete system is made up of at least two substances and a field that affects them in the desired way.

Sufield Analysis with Complete Systems

Example:

Using a compactor (S_2) which deploys mechanical force (F), metal parts (S_1) are brought into the desired shape.

2. **Incomplete systems**

   Systems are incomplete when one or more components are missing. The desired effect cannot be generated.

Sufield Analysis with Incomplete Systems

Example:
The consistence of a refrigerator's cooling unit is to be examined. A fluorescent substance is mixed into the cooling liquid and the unit radiated with ultraviolet light in a dark room. Leaks become visible.

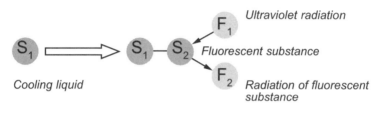

Incomplete systems must be completed to achieve the desired effect.

3. **Complete but inefficient systems**
   Complete systems are inefficient when their intended effect does not reach the desired degree.

Sufield Analysis with Complete but Inefficient Systems

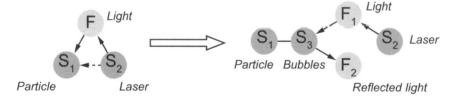

Example:
Optically complete clear fluids are to be examined to see if there are any impurities. Because these impurities are non-magnetic particles, a laser is used to scan the fluid. However, some of these particles are so small that they are unable to provide a good reflection of the light. By heating the fluid the surrounding particles begin to boil. The resulting bubbles can be detected easily.

Inefficient systems must be improved.

DEFINE

MEASURE

ANALYZE

DESIGN

VERIFY

DEFINE

MEASURE

ANALYZE

DESIGN

VERIFY

4. Complete but harmful systems

A harmful interaction takes place between the components in these systems.

Sufield Analysis with Complete but Harmful Systems

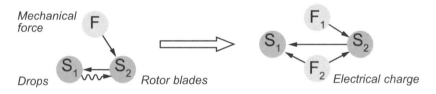

Example:

The rotor blades of steam turbines are surrounded by a mixture of steam and water drops. Relatively large drops (between 50 and 800 µm in diameter) collide with the rapidly rotating blades, damaging their surface. The rotor blades and the water drops are therefore charged with the same electrical potential. They reject one another.

The negative effects of a harmful system must be eliminated.

TRIZ literature describes 76 standard solutions as aids for solving abstracted problems.

76 Standard Solutions

📋 **Term/Description**
76 Standard Solutions

🕗 **When**
In the Analyze and Design Phases, optimizing the design concept

◎ **Goal**
Eliminate incomplete functional structures

▶▶ **Steps**
The 76 standard solutions may be arranged thematically into the following five groups:
1. Composition and decomposition of complete Sufield models
2. Improvement of Sufield models
3. Transition to super and subsystems (macro and micro levels)
4. Detection and measurement
5. Aids for applying standards

The 76 standard solutions in overview

1.   Composition and decomposition of complete Sufield models
1.1   Composition of Sufield models (SFM)
1.1.1   Complete an incomplete SFM
1.1.2   Complete when an internal additive can be used
1.1.3   Complete when an external additive can be used
1.1.4   Use resources for completion
1.1.5   Generate further resources by changing the system environment
1.1.6   Use surplus activities to complete and then eliminate the surplus
1.1.7   If the surplus action is harmful attempt to direct it to other components in the system
1.1.8   Introduce local protective substances for completion

1.2   Decomposition of Sufield models
1.2.1   Eliminate harmful interactions by introducing a third substance, S_3

1.2.2 Eliminate harmful interactions by introducing a third substance, S_3, whereby S_3 can be a modification of the existing substances, S_1 and / or S_2

1.2.3 Direct the effect onto a less important substance, S_3

1.2.4 Introduce a new field to compensate harmful effects

1.2.5 Turn a magnetic field on or off according to need

2. Improvement of the Sufield models

2.1 Transition to complex Sufield models

2.2 Interlink several SFMs

2.3 Duplicate a SFM

2.2 Further development of a Sufield model

2.2.1 Employ fields which can be controlled more easily

2.2.2 Fragment S_2

2.2.3 Deploy capillaries and porous substances

2.2.4 Increase the level of dynamics

2.2.5 Structured fields (e.g. stationary waves)

2.2.6 Structured substances (e.g. ferroconcrete)

2.3 Rhythm coordination

2.3.1 Bring into agreement the rhythm (frequency) of the affecting field with one of the two substances (or controlled non-agreement)

2.3.2 Synchronize the rhythm, the frequency of fields

2.3.3 Bring independent actions into a rhythmic connection

2.4 Complex improved Sufield models

2.4.1 Use ferromagnetic substances and magnetic fields

2.4.2 Use ferromagnetic particles, granules, powders

2.4.3 Use ferromagnetic liquids

2.4.4 Use capillary structures in combination with ferromagnetism

2.4.5 Use complex ferromagnetic SFMs, e.g. external magnetic fields, ferromagnetic additives etc.

2.4.6 Introduce ferromagnetic material into the system environment if it is unable to magnetize itself

2.4.7 Use natural effects (e.g. Curie point)

2.4.8 Use dynamic, variable or self-adapting magnetic fields

2.4.9 Change the structure of a material by incorporating ferromagnetic particles and applying a magnetic field to move the particles

2.4.10 Calibrate the rhythms

2.4.11 Use electrical current instead of ferromagnetic particles to generate magnetic fields

2.4.12 Use electrorheology

3. Transition into super and subsystems (macro and micro levels)

3.1 Transition into bi and poly systems

3.1.1 Combine systems into bi and poly systems

3.1.2 Create or intensify the connections between the individual elements in bi and poly systems

3.1.3 Improve the efficiency of bi and poly systems by enlarging the difference between individual components

3.1.4 Simplify bi and poly systems by eliminating superfluous, redundant or similar components

3.1.5 Opposite attributes of the whole system and individual components

3.2 Transition to micro systems

3.2.1 Miniaturized components or whole systems

4. Detection and measurement

4.1 Indirect methods

4.1.1 Avoid detection and measurement

4.1.2 Carry out detection and measurement on a copy

4.1.3 Replace measurement with two successive detection procedures

4.2 Composition of Sufield models for measuring

4.2.1 Detect or measure using an additional field

4.2.2 Introduce additives, substances that can be easily detected and measured

4.2.3 Introduce fields into the system environment which can be easily detected and measured if nothing can be added to the system

4.2.4 If additives cannot be introduced into the system environment change the state of something that is already present in the system environment and measure the effect of the system on this changed substance / object

4.3 Improvement of measurement systems

4.3.1 Use natural effects to improve measurement systems

4.3.2 Use resonance phenomena for measurement

4.3.3 Use objects linked by resonance phenomena for (indirect) measurement

4.4 **Transition to ferromagnetic measurement systems (this was a popular method before the introduction of microprocessors and fiber optics etc.)**
4.4.1   Deploy ferromagnetic substances and magnetic fields
4.4.2   Replace substances with ferromagnetic substances and detect or measure via the magnetic field
4.4.3   Generate complex, linked SFMs with ferromagnetic components
4.4.4   Introduce ferromagnetic materials into the system environment
4.4.5   Use the impact of naturally magnetic effects for measurement

4.5 **Evolution of detection and measurement**
4.5.1   Generate bi and poly systems
4.5.2   Detect and measure the first and second derivations in time and space instead of the original functions (e.g. changes in frequency instead of speed [Doppler effect])

5. **Aids for applying standards**
5.1 **Introduce substances**
5.1.1   Indirect methods (e.g. introduce vacuums or cavities as substances)
5.1.2   Divide the elements into smaller units
5.1.3   Use the self-elimination of substances
5.1.4   Use the substances abundantly

5.2 **Introduce fields**
5.2.1   Use a field to trigger the generation of another field
5.2.2   Use fields from the system environment
5.2.3   Use substances of generating fields (e.g. magnetic substances)

5.3 **Phase transitions**
5.3.1   Change the aggregate state or the phase of substances
5.3.2   Use two aggregate states or phases of a substance
5.3.3   Use the physical effects accompanying a phase transition
5.3.4   Use effects which result from the simultaneous presence of two phases (e.g. use "phase transitive" metals)
5.3.5   Improve the interaction between the elements or phases of a system

5.4 **Use natural phenomena**
5.4.1   Use self-controlled, reversible physical transformations
5.4.2   Use storage or amplifying effects

5.5   Substance particles

5.5.1   Generate substance particles (e.g. ions) by decomposing more complex structured substances (e.g. molecules)

5.5.2   Generate substance particles (e.g. atoms) by combining less complex structured substances (elementary particles)

5.5.3   If a substance cannot be decomposed begin to decompose on the second highest substance level. If it is not possible to combine substance particles begin to combine on the next highest substance level.

DEFINE

MEASURE

ANALYZE

DESIGN

VERIFY

DEFINE

MEASURE

ANALYZE

DESIGN

VERIFY

Trimming – Complexity Reduction

▢ **Term/Description**
Trimming

🕑 **When**
In the Analyze and Design Phases, optimizing the design concept

◎ **Goal**
Simplify the system by eliminating individual components

▶▶ **Steps**
Experience shows that technical systems with a high degree of complexity are principally less reliable than simpler ones. It also makes sense to reduce the complexity of a system. This is achieved by trimming: individual system components are made superfluous and eliminated.

Reducing parts and complexity by trimming

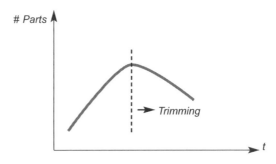

Suitable for trimming are those components whose value are low for the system anyway. The Functional Analysis and Value Engineering, an approach developed by Lawrence Miles, help to identify these trimming candidates.
According to this approach the value of a component or a subsystem is determined by the relation of its functionality to its costs:

$$\text{Value} = \frac{\text{Functionality}}{\text{Costs}}$$

The functionality of a system component is defined by the proportion of its contribution to the overall function as well as its relationship to the system's other components.

Detecting the Trimming candidates to be eliminated
Value engineering evaluation matrix

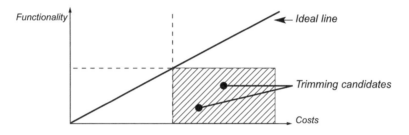

Components placed in the bottom right quadrant of the matrix have the lowest value for the system. The aim is to make these trimming candidates superfluous and to remove them from the system.

Detecting the trimming candidates to be optimized
Value engineering evaluation matrix

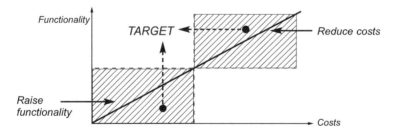

If a component is in the upper right quadrant of the matrix its costs must be cut. If a component is in the lower left quadrant its functionality must be raised.

DEFINE

MEASURE

ANALYZE

DESIGN

VERIFY

To determine the relative functionality of a system component the following steps are to be undertaken:

1. Determine the main function of the system

2. Draw up a functional model of the system

3. The components are sequenced according to their distance from the main function. The component most distant from the main function is given the lowest functional ranking 1.

4. The functional ranking of the respective components is multiplied by the number of their functions (= absolute functionality).

5. The relative functionality is gained by dividing the absolute functionality of the individual components through the aggregate of all absolute functionalities.

Determining the relative functionality
Example: functionality of the components in a toothbrush

❶ *The main function of a toothbrush is to remove plaque from teeth*

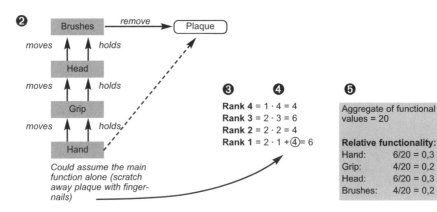

❷ Brushes — remove → Plaque
moves / holds
Head
moves / holds
Grip
moves / holds
Hand
Could assume the main function alone (scratch away plaque with fingernails)

❸
Rank 4 = 1 · 4 = 4
Rank 3 = 2 · 3 = 6
Rank 2 = 2 · 2 = 4
Rank 1 = 2 · 1 + ④ = 6

❹

❺
Aggregate of functional values = 20

Relative functionality:
Hand: 6/20 = 0,3
Grip: 4/20 = 0,2
Head: 6/20 = 0,3
Brushes: 4/20 = 0,2

These relative functionalities allow the system components to be sorted into an evaluation matrix. The components suitable for trimming actions can be determined due their unfavorable value (functionality-cost relation).

Now the question for these trimming candidates is:
How can they be made superfluous for the system and eliminated from it?
And how can the remaining system components take over the individual
functions without adversely affecting the total function?

DEFINE

MEASURE

ANALYZE

DESIGN

VERIFY

Evolution of Technological Systems

📁 **Term / Description**
Evolution of Technological Systems

🕒 **When**
In the Analyze and Design Phases, optimizing the design concept

◎ **Goal**
Predict the future evolution steps of a technology to push system development forward in a targeted way

▶▶ **Steps**
Like biological systems, technological systems move through four typical evolution phases:

1. **Infancy**
   Phase prior to entering the market, system evolves rather slowly

2. **Rapid growth**
   Entering the market, the speed of evolution accelerates rapidly

3. **Maturity**
   The system is established, the system's evolution slows down and ceases

4. **Decline**
   A new system takes the place of the old one

The relation between costs and benefits of a system is subject to corresponding changes and in a chart takes the form of an S in the course of the four phases.

An S-Curve Analysis is presented on the following page.

DEFINE

S-Curve Analysis

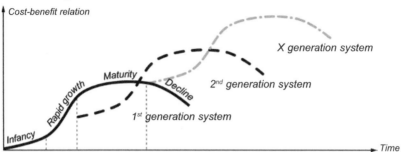

A timely entry into a new system generation has to be found if a constantly growing cost-benefit relation is to be achieved.

In line with the positioning of the system on the s-curve graph, two fundamental questions arise:

1. Which changes need to be made to the system to advance its position on the s-curve?
2. How could the new generation of the system/technology look like?

The nine laws of evolution for technological systems can provide the answers to these questions.

MEASURE

ANALYZE

Nine laws of evolution for technological systems

1. Law of increasing ideality of systems
2. Law of non-uniform development of subsystems
3. Law of transition to super systems
4. Law of increasing flexibility of systems
5. Law of transition from the macro to the micro level
6. Law of shortening energy flow in systems
7. Law of harmonizing of rhythm in systems
8. Law of increasing automation of systems
9. Law of increasing controllability of systems

DESIGN

VERIFY

DEFINE

MEASURE

ANALYZE

DESIGN

VERIFY

1. **Law of increasing ideality**

   This law says that technological systems always evolve in the direction of increasing ideality:
   - The disadvantages of the original (old) system are eliminated
   - The positive attributes of the original system are kept
   - The new system is not more complicated than the original system
   - No new disadvantages are added to the new system

   The degree of ideality is determined by the relation between functionality and expense.

   $$\text{The degree of ideality} = \frac{\text{Functionality}}{\text{Effort (e.g. €, energy, weight, etc.)}}$$

Law 1

Example: the development of home appliances

Home appliances	Price in USD 1947	Price in USD 1997	Improved functionality
Refrigerator	1470	700	Twice as large; ice machine
Washing machine	1770	380	Quieter; improved energy efficiency
Television	3180 (black & white)	300	Color image; stereo sound; remote control

2. **Law of non-uniform development of subsystems**

   This law says that the different components of a technical system are always in different stages of development.
   For this reason there are always components which are behind other subsystems (their position on the s-curve) in terms of their development level. The more complex a system, the less uniform is the stage of development of its components. The resulting contradictions emerging in the system have to be resolved if the development process is to be pushed forward.

DEFINE

MEASURE

ANALYZE

DESIGN

VERIFY

Law 2

Example: stages of development in computer technology

PC
*(monitor and key-
board separate)*

Laptop
*(monitor and key-
board integrated)*

Mini laptop

*Minicomputer with-
out keyboard*

The miniaturization of electronic components in computer technology (from conductor to micro electronics) has enabled a massive reduction in the size of appliances. However, this potential to decrease size can only be exploited if the control and presentation concepts (keyboard and monitor) are also developed further.

3. Law of transition to super-systems

This law says that technological systems generally evolve from mono to bi or poly systems.
The integration of two independent mono systems generates a more complex bi system

Law 3

Example: development of hi-fi systems

Cassette recorder   *CD player*   *Radio*   *Record player*

Hi-fi system with all 4 components

DEFINE

MEASURE

ANALYZE

Especially in the mature phase of systems additional functions are added to enhance their attractiveness. If a system is able to fulfill a large number of additional functions this is a good indicator that it has already exceeded its evolutionary peak and will soon be replaced by a new technology.

4. Law of increasing flexibility

This law says that technological systems develop increasingly flexible structures and in this way always become increasingly adaptable.
Increasing flexibility can be achieved in two different ways:
1. Increasing the flexibility of the function in a system
2. Increasing the flexibility of the structure in a system

Increasing flexibility of a system function

Increasing flexibility of a system structure

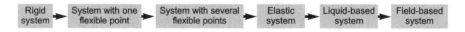

DESIGN

Law 4
*Example: car steering wheels**

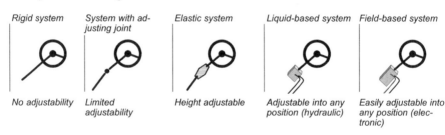

Rigid system	System with adjusting joint	Elastic system	Liquid-based system	Field-based system
No adjustability	Limited adjustability	Height adjustable	Adjustable into any position (hydraulic)	Easily adjustable into any position (electronic)

VERIFY

* *Cf. Bernd Gimpel, et. al. (2000): Ideen finden. Produkte entwickeln mit TRIZ. Hanser Verlag, Munich/Vienna, p. 105.*

5. **Law of transition from the macro to the micro level**

   The tasks of a technological system previously taken over by macro objects are increasingly fulfilled by micro objects.

Transition from the macro to the micro level

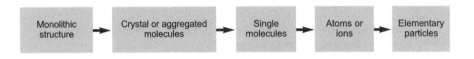

   The advantage here is enhanced controllability, often in connection with increased functionality (e.g. evident in a comparison between mechanical and digital watches).

   The micro structures of a system can take over different tasks:
   - Micro structures can take over functions previously performed by macro structures
     Example:
   - By replacing traditional mechanical cutting tools with laser photons micro structures control the physical attributes and the behavior of macro structures.
     Example·
     Spectacle lenses with photochrome particles which alter their translucence depending on the solar radiation.

6. **Law of shortening energy flow in systems**

   This law says that the distance to be covered by the energy in a technological system is reduced over the generations.

   In the most effective system the energy source directly impacts the working appliance:

DEFINE

MEASURE

ANALYZE

DESIGN

VERIFY

Energy flow in a technological system

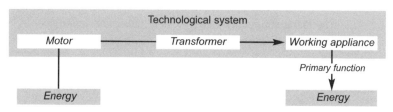

The trend to ever shorter energy flows within systems is evident in the development of industrial machines.
Around 1920 energy was still directed from a central motor via drive shafts and belts to the individual machines, from the 1930s onwards a separate electric motor was installed in the individual machines, shortening the distance the energy had to cover through the system.

7. Law of harmonizing rhythm

This law says that the effectiveness of a technological system is raised through the increasing harmonization / synchronization of the movements of all its parts. Harmonization can be achieved in three different ways:
1. Coordinate the temporal sequences of moving system components
2. Utilize resonance
3. Eliminate undesired temporal sequences

Examples:
– An aircraft needs a coordinated control of movements (adjust and align the different control vanes). While this used to occur manually, coordination in modern machines was improved by using computers ("fly-by-wire").
– Airbrush pistols need a coordinated opening and closing of the air and paint valves to ensure that no paint drips onto the surface to be processed.

8. Law of increasing automation

This law says that the degree of automation increases as a technological system evolves.

Functions originally performed by man are taken over by a system that developes as follows:

1. Man performs the function
2. Shift to tool functions
3. Shift to transition functions
4. Shift the function of the energy source
5. Shift the control functions

Law 8

Example: increasing automation of systems

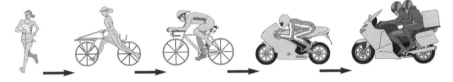

9. Law of increasing controllability

This law says the controllability of a technological system constantly improves because the Sufield interactions within and outside this system continually increase.

Law 9

Example: development of cooking area

Improving the Sufield interaction is achieved in the following ways:

1. Replace an uncontrollable field or one which is difficult to control with a controllable one (e.g. a field based on gravity with a mechanical field, or a mechanical one with an electromagnetic field).
2. Raise the degree of flexibility of the elements in a Sufield interaction.
3. Adjust the field frequency to the natural frequency of the object or tool.

DEFINE

MEASURE

ANALYZE

DESIGN

VERIFY

Deriving Requirements to Necessary Resources

☐ **Term / Description**
Identification of necessary resources

🕐 **When**
In the Analyze and Design Phases

◎ **Goal**
Clarify the resources necessary for a detailed further development of the concept

▶▶ **Steps**
Identifying the necessary resources occurs on the basis of the defined conflict-free concept design. Using descriptive specifications, sketches, computer visualizations and already existing prototypes, the necessary resources can be identified systematically and can be requested in time.

The following resources are necessary for developing the detailed design:
− Time
− Money
− Manpower (skills and numbers)
− Equipment, materials, machines, etc.

The activities, schedule, and resource planning (see Define Phase) have to be updated and detailed at this point.

Reviewing the Capability of the Concept

📁 **Term / Description**
Proof of Concept, feasibility study

🕐 **When**
Closure of the Analyze Phase

◎ **Goals**
- Estimate risks by identifying possible weaknesses in the design concept
- Minimize risks by introducing counter-measures in due time

▶▶ **Steps**
As the design concept's level of detail increases, the costs incurred through undetected weaknesses of the design rise exponentially.

Costs of undetected weaknesses in the design concept

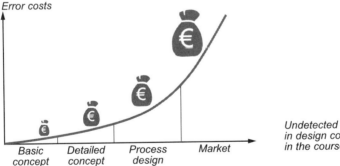

Error costs

Basic concept   Detailed concept   Process design   Market

Undetected weaknesses in design concept in the course of time

Weaknesses in the design concept should be detected and eliminated as soon as possible. For this purpose internal and external risks are to be estimated. The concept itself must be reviewed and tested with suitable methods and must be subject to detailed customer feedback.

DEFINE

MEASURE

ANALYZE

DESIGN

VERIFY

DEFINE

MEASURE

ANALYZE

DESIGN

VERIFY

Risk Evaluation

📁 **Term / Description**

Risk evaluation

🕐 **When**

In the Analyze and Design Phases, reviewing the capability of the concept, evaluating the risk

◎ **Goals**

- Identify existing and potential weak points in the design concept
- Take suitable counter measures

▶▶ **Steps**

A concept FMEA (Failure Mode and Effect Analysis) is a suitable tool for identifying possible weaknesses in the prioritized concept early, i.e. before the detailed design of the system.

Here every process step / function is examined for possible errors and their potential effects to enable the initiation of counter measures.

Another tool is the Anticipatory Failure Detection (AFD), which identifies potential errors in advance and presents preventive measures.

Failure Mode and Effect Analysis (FMEA)

📁 **Term / Description**
FMEA, Failure Mode and Effect Analysis

🕐 **When**
In the Analyze and Design Phases

◎ **Goal**
Detect any weaknesses when developing the product or process early and derive countermeasures.

▶▶ **Steps**
Conducting an FMEA comprises 5 steps.

The 5 FMEA Steps

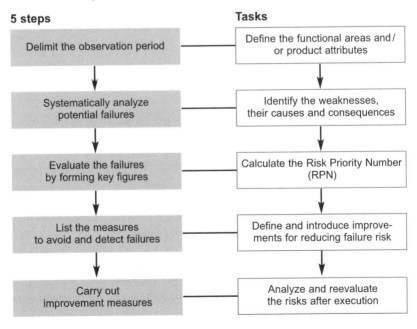

5 steps	Tasks
Delimit the observation period	Define the functional areas and / or product attributes
Systematically analyze potential failures	Identify the weaknesses, their causes and consequences
Evaluate the failures by forming key figures	Calculate the Risk Priority Number (RPN)
List the measures to avoid and detect failures	Define and introduce improvements for reducing failure risk
Carry out improvement measures	Analyze and reevaluate the risks after execution

DEFINE

MEASURE

ANALYZE

DESIGN

VERIFY

DEFINE

MEASURE

ANALYZE

DESIGN

VERIFY

Process/ Product: ❶									FMEA date: Original						
FMEA Team:									Changed:						
Black Belt:									Page:						

FMEA Process												**Results**				
Position Function Process step	Potential failure opportunity	Potential effect(s) of failure	Severity	Potential cause(s)/ mecha- nisms of failure	Frequency	Current controls/ management	Detection	RPN	Recom- mended action	Responsi- bilities & conclusion date	Measures taken		Severity	Frequency	Detection	RPN
❷	❸	❹	❺	❻	❼	❽	❾	❿	⓫	⓬	⓭		⓮	⓯	⓰	⓱

❶ Note down general information about the project in the documentation sheet.

❷ Describe in detail the analyzed process or the analyzed product function.

❸ Describe the potential failure modes: why did the process/product fail to meet the requirements demanded by a specific operation?

❹ Depict the effect the failure mode/failure has on the output.

❺ Estimate the severity of the effect generated by the potential failure mode.

❻ List the potential causes of the failure or the mechanisms triggering the failure.

❼ Estimate the frequency with which the cause of the failure occurs while the process is carried out.

❽ Specify the opportunities for identifying the failure cause or for avoiding its occurrence.

❾ Estimate the probability of detecting a potential cause before the hand-over to the next process step takes place.

❿ Calculate the product of the severity, frequency, and detection proba-bility. The rating scale, resulting from the RPN (Risk Priority Number), prioritizes the fields of action. If the RPN is high, more detailed analy-sis is required.

DEFINE

⓫ Define the actions which mainly reduce the rating of frequency and / or detection probability to reduce the overall RPNs.

⓬ Name the responsible persons and set the closure date.

⓭ Describe the measures actually taken and set the implementation date.

⓮ Estimate the effect of a potential failure mode on the customer after the improvement measure has been implemented.

⓯ Estimate the frequency with which the failure cause occurs during the execution of the process after the improvement measure has been implemented.

⓰ Estimate the probability of detecting a potential cause before the hand-over to the next process step occurs after the improvement measure has been implemented.

⓱ Recalculate the RPN.

MEASURE

ANALYZE

	Rating Scale: Severity
1	Remains unnoticed and has no effect
2	Remains unnoticed and has only an insignificant effect
3	Causes only minor inconvenience
4	Causes a minor loss of performance
5	Causes a loss of performance which results in a customer complaint
6	Causes a loss of performance which results in breakdown of functionality
7	Defective functionality results in enormous customer dissatisfaction
8	Product or service becomes unusable
9	Product or service is illegal
10	Customer or employee is injured or killed

DESIGN

VERIFY

DEFINE

MEASURE

ANALYZE

DESIGN

VERIFY

Rating Scale: Frequency	
1	Every 100 years
2	Every 5-100 years
3	Every 3-5 years
4	Every 1-3 years
5	Every year
6	Every 6 months
7	Once per month
8	Once per week
9	Once per day
10	Several times per day

Rating Scale: Detection probability	
1	Failure cause is obvious and can be easily prevented
2	All units are inspected automatically
3	Statistical process control with systematic examination and prevention measures for failure causes
4	Statistical process control is carried out with systematic examination of failure causes
5	Statistical process control is carried out
6	All units are checked manually and prevention measures for failure causes are installed
7	All units are checked manually
8	Frequent manual examination of failure causes
9	Occasional manual examination of failure causes
10	The failure cannot be detected

Concept FMEA

Example: passenger seat

Concept FMEA										Results				
Position Function Process step	Potential failure opportunity	Potential effect(s) of failure	Severity	Potential mecha-nisms of failure	Frequency	Current controls/ management	Detection	RPN	Recom-mended action	Responsi-bilities & conclusion date	Measures taken	Severity	Frequency	Detection	RPN
Holding rail	Dirt & grime	Difficult instal-lation	6	Stones, sand, etc	10		9	540							
	Accident	Seats loosened from mounting	10		7	Driver training	10	700							
Frame	Fluids	Corrosion	8	Water, acids	8		8	512							
Joint frame/ seat	Simple disas-sembly	Theft	5		10		8	400							
	Accident	Seats loosened from mounting	10		7	Driver training	10	700							
Synthetic shell of seat	Vandalism	Sharp edges	10	Knives, breakage	8		8	640							
	Spilt fluids	Damage	5	Water, acids	8		8	320							

Excerpt

⇨ **Tips**

- The evaluation of the RPN is always branch-specific and firm-specific.
- Nonetheless, there is generally a need for action if the RPN is > 125.
- Reducing the RPN or the corresponding failure potential of a function can be primarily achieved by actions which influence the frequency and/or the detection probability.
- The FMEA is supplemented by actions with assigned responsibilities, a renewed evaluation of frequency, and detection probability, and a con-cluding calculation of the RPN.
- An FMEA can be used for a variety of purposes:
  - Concept FMEA
  - Design FMEA
  - Process FMEA
  - System FMEA
  - Subsystem FMEA
  - Components FMEA
  - Assembly/Installation FMEA
  - Production FMEA
  - Machine FMEA
- The basic approach is identical for all applications.

DEFINE MEASURE ANALYZE DESIGN VERIFY

Anticipatory Failure Detection

⬜ **Term / Description**

Anticipatory Failure Detection, subversive failure analysis

🕐 **When**

In the Analyze and Design Phases

◎ **Goal**

Anticipatory identification of potential failures and preventive measures

▶▶ **Steps**

An Anticipatory Failure Detection (AFD) can be an effective means to detect potential failure sources in new technologies and systems.

Here failures are provoked intentionally whereby the following questions are posed:
- How can the breakdown of the system be brought about?
- Which available resources from the system and its environment can be used to sabotage the system?

The reason for the breakdown is transformed into a desired function. Individual TRIZ and Poka Yoke methods can then be applied to an inverted problem. The defective function – in the sense of "how can this failure be generated?"– is inverted into the primary beneficial function of the system. Subsequently the attempt is undertaken to generate this "beneficial function" through the given system and environment conditions.

An Anticipatory Failure Detection includes 4 steps.

DEFINE

Anticipatory Failure Detection

1. Define the target functions	Define the target function per component with subsequent inverting: what has to happen or be done to disable the target function? The inverted problem has to be reinforced further.
2. Define resources	Define the available resources (material, spacial, temporal, etc.) which can contribute to the breakdown. Resources can be from the system as well as its environment.
3. Overcome contradictions	Search for solutions with the aid of TRIZ methods: formulate technological and physical contradictions, 40 innovative principles, ARIZ etc.
4. Avoid failures	Selected failure opportunities are now converted back to actual problems. Measures for avoiding these failures (Poka Yoke) are then defined.

MEASURE

⇨ **Tips**
- The Anticipatory Failure Detection is also suitable as a preparation for an FMEA and the analysis of linked failures and chains of failures.
- Thinking barriers are broken through and subjective thinking is reduced.
- Inverting the problem generates useful information because the inverted perspective reveals aspects about the system and its environment which would not emerge in a conventional approach, which is problem-oriented.

ANALYZE

DESIGN

VERIFY

225

DEFINE

MEASURE

ANALYZE

DESIGN

VERIFY

Getting Customer and Stakeholder Feed-back

☐ **Term / Description**
Receive customer and stakeholder feedback

🕑 **When**
In the Analyze and Design Phases, examining the capability of the concept

◎ **Goal**
Possible adaptation of the selected and optimized best design concept to subjective customer feedback

▸▸ **Steps**
Representative target customers and important stakeholders are invited to judge the developed concept.
The team presents the status of the project:
– Short presentation of the approach and course of the project up to this point (MS Power Point presentation)
– If necessary integration of computer-supported visualization (CAD / CAM)
– If necessary presentation of a prototype
– Etc.

Each person invited to the session gives his subjective feedback. The feedback is then analyzed and if necessary changes are implemented in the design concept.

226

Finalizing the Concept

📁 **Term / Description**
Finalize the design concept, freeze the concept

🕐 **When**
In the Analyze and Design Phases, examining the capability of the concept

◎ **Goal**
Systematically analyze and elaborate customer feedback to finalize the concept

▶▶ **Steps**
Analyzing customer feedback should be oriented towards the following primary aspects:
  – If several concepts were presented the key question is:
    Is there a clearly preferred concept?
  – If there is such a preference the following should be clarified:
  – From the the customer's point of view what are the critical attributes of the concept which make it "valuable" or useful?
  – Are further reviews, tests, or surveys necessary to clarify possible fears and / or risks?

These possible risks can be documented in an adjusted Risk Management Matrix.

A Risk Management Matrix is presented on the following page.

DEFINE

MEASURE

ANALYZE

DESIGN

VERIFY

DEFINE

MEASURE

ANALYZE

DESIGN

VERIFY

Risk Management Matrix

High	Moderate risk	High risk	Show stopper
Moderate	Low risk	Moderate risk	High risk
Low	Low risk	Low risk	Moderate risk
	Low	Moderate	High

Probability of occurrence

Influence on project success

☐ *Reduce before continuing the project or stop the project*

▨ *Minimize or control risks*

☐ *Proceed with caution*

Scaling probability of occurrence and influence

Scaling	Probability of occurrence	Influence
High	• Major concerns / existing risks • Extensive concept changes necessary • No statements on concept suitability possible – no data available	Changes with regard to performance, quality, costs and / or safety lead to *extensive* concept adjustments and delays in the project plan
Moderate	• Some concerns / existing risks • Moderate concept changes necessary • Some statements on concept suitability possible – data exists	Changes with regard to performance, quality, costs and / or safety lead to *minor* concept adjustments and delays in the project plan
Low	• No concerns / existing risks • No concept changes necessary • Extensive statements on concept suitability possible – extensive data available	Changes with regard to performance, quality, costs and / or safety do *not* lead to any concept adjustments and delays in the project plan

DEFINE

This form of systematic elaboration can serve as the basis for discussions and decision-making as to whether to proceed to the Design Phase or to adjust the presented concept once again.

Responsibility for possible adjustments to the concept design has to be clarified and the timeframe for these adjustments has to be set.

If there is no clear preference for one of the presented concepts, the following question needs to be clarified: are there preferred attributes within the presented concepts which can be combined to generate an optimum?

It is essential to determine if a further concept review is necessary.

MEASURE

ANALYZE

DESIGN

VERIFY

DEFINE

MEASURE

ANALYZE

DESIGN

VERIFY

Preparing Market Launch

⬛ Term / Description
Market launch, strategy for introducing the product to the market, market positioning

🕑 When
In the Analyze and Design Phases

◎ Goal
Ensure a successful market launch

▶▶ Steps
Of key importance for a successful market launch is the right positioning of the product in the market. For this purpose the positioning of competitors and the evaluation of the competitive situation by potential customers must be taken into consideration.

Representative target customers are to compare the developed product concept / design model with the products of competitors.

The specific product attributes are evaluated and positioned in line with the competitive advantage matrix.

DEFINE

Competitive Advantage Matrix: market positioning

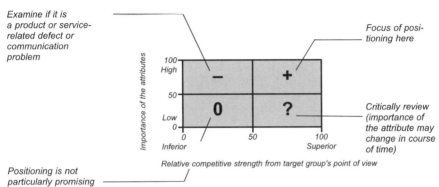

Examine if it is a product or service-related defect or communication problem

Focus of positioning here

Critically review (importance of the attribute may change in course of time)

Positioning is not particularly promising

Relative competitive strength from target group's point of view

MEASURE

The focus for a corresponding marketing strategy can be derived from this positioning. As a rule, a successful marketing strategy comprises four areas.

The 4 Ps of a Marketing Strategy

ANALYZE

Product	Price
• Layout/packaging • Branding • Service	• (List) prices • Discounts/conditions • Price policy strategies over time
Place	Promotion
• Sales area • Sales channels • Sales agents • Logistics	• Advertising, PR • Sales & promotion campaign • Personal selling

Depending on the economic sector, different marketing instruments are utilized within these areas.*

DESIGN

*   Cf. Meffert, Heribert (1998): Marketing – Grundlagen marktorientierter Unternehmensführung, p. 891. 8th edition, Gabler, Wiesbaden, ISBN 3-409-69015-8.

VERIFY

231

DEFINE

MEASURE

ANALYZE

DESIGN

VERIFY

Marketing Strategies* according to the economic sectors

Sales policy instruments		Investment goods		Consumer goods		Services	
		Companies producing raw materials	Manufacturing companies of finished products	Manufacturer of branded articles	Manufacturer of trademarks	Commerce	Other
Product	• Product quality	●	●	●			●
	• Range of products		●	●			●
	• Guarantees		●	●		●	
	• Customer service		●	●		●	●
Price	• Price			●	●	●	
	• Discounts			●	●	●	
	• Terms of payment	●	●				
Place	• Location of final sales point			●	●	●	●
	• Sales channels			●			
	• Readiness to deliver, physical distribution	●	●	●		●	●
Promotion	• "Classic advertising"	●		●		●	●
	• Promotion campaign			●		●	●
	• Public relations	●	●	●			
	• Direct advertising						●
	• Sales policy activity level	Very small	Small	Very big	Very small	Very big	Big

* Cf. Meffert, Heribert (1998): Marketing – Grundlagen marktorientierter Unternehmensführung, p. 891. 8th edition, Gabler, Wiesbaden, ISBN 3-409-69015-8.

Gate Review

📁 **Term / Description**
Gate Review, phase check

🕑 **When**
At the conclusion of each phase

◎ **Goals**
- Inform the Sponsor about the results and measures of the respective phase
- Assess the results
- Decide on the further course of the project

▸▸ **Steps**
The results are presented completely and in an easily comprehensible form.
The Sponsor is to examine the current status of the project on the basis of the following criteria:
- Results are complete,
- Probability of project success,
- Resources are optimally allocated in the project.

The Sponsor decides if the project can enter the next phase.

All of the results from the Analyze Phase are presented to the Sponsor and Stakeholders in the Analyze Gate Review. The following questions must be answered in a complete and comprehensible presentation:

DEFINE

MEASURE

ANALYZE

DESIGN

VERIFY

233

DEFINE

MEASURE

ANALYZE

DESIGN

VERIFY

Identifying the design concept:
- Were the product/process functions formulated clearly and completely? What are they?
- Which design concepts were drawn up?
- To what extent was the Multigeneration Plan (MGP) complied with? What influence will the design concept have on following generations?
- To what degree were customers or stakeholders involved in the development process so far?
- How was the prioritized concept selected?
- Was a concept FMEA carried out? If so, which changes were made to the selected concept as a result?
- What are the strengths and weaknesses of the selected concept?
- Was a benchmarking carried out? If so, what was the result?
- What distinguishes the concept from our competitors?

Optimizing the design concept:
- Were (occurring) contradictions identified and resolved innovatively? If so, how?
- Were the resources necessary for developing the design identified? To what extent and when are these available?
- Were the target costs kept? What are the primary cost drivers?

Reviewing the concept capability:
- Was the selected concept evaluated on the basis of customer feedback? What is the result?
- Which risks need to be considered?

On managing the project:
- Was it necessary to adjust the Business Case?
- Was the project plan adjusted? Can design activities be accelerated if required?
- Should the project be continued?
- What are the lessons learned from the Analyze Phase?
- What are the next steps in the project?

Design for Six Sigma^{+Lean} Toolset

DESIGN

DEFINE

MEASURE

ANALYZE

DESIGN

VERIFY

Phase 4: Design

Goals

- Detail the system design to completely and predictably fulfill all specifications and functions
- Examine and review target production
- Develop and prepare the lean process

Developing, testing, optimizing the detailed concept	Testing performance capability for target production	Developing and optimizing the lean process
• Formulate Transfer Function • Generate and compare alternative design elements • Apply tolerance design and design for X • Develop a scorecard for the detailed design • Test the detailed concept • Select the detailed concept • Adjust the design scorecard • Estimate risks • Avoid risks	• Identify relevant process and input variables • Evaluate current performance capability	• Create the process design • Draw up SOPs • Plan facilities and buildings • Plan equipment • Plan material procurement • Ensure employees are available • Provide necessary IT • Optimize the lean process design

Steps

After finalization of the detailed concept the existing production process is to be reviewed, or if necessary a new process is developed. Furthermore, all necessary process and input variables for the new production process are identified and specified.

A roadmap for the Design Phase is presented on the opposite page.

Most Important Tools

- Transfer Function
- Zigzag Diagram
- QFD 3
- Tree Diagram
- Creativity Techniques
- Tolerance Design
- Prototyping

- Statistical procedures (hypothesis tests, DOE)
- Design Scorecard
- FMEA
- QFD 4
- Pugh Matrix
- Simulation

- Lean Toolbox (incl. Value Stream, Pull Systems, Poka Yoke)
- CIT
- Process Management Diagram

Design Roadmap

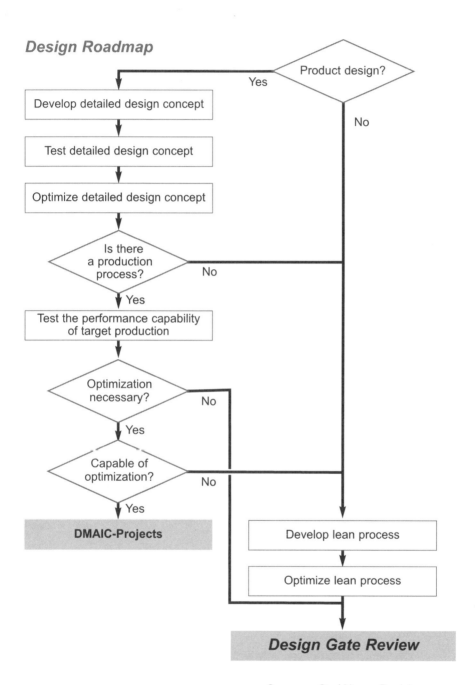

Sponsor: Go / No-go Decision

DEFINE

MEASURE

ANALYZE

DESIGN

VERIFY

Develop, Test and Optimize Detailed Design

🗁 Term / Description
Develop, test and optimize detailed design

🕐 When
At the beginning of the Design Phase

◎ Goals
- Develop a detailed design concept capable of implementation
- Fulfill the specifications through a stable, predictable and capable process

▶▶ Steps
When developing the detailed design the basic concept selected in the Analyze Phase is further elaborated and refined.

From basic concept to detailed design

Analyze Phase	**Design Phase**
Basic design concept	Detailed design concept
	Level of detail
Low	High

The relation between the specific attributes of the design elements and the system functions is to be determined in the Design Phase (transfer function).

With the aid of known creativity techniques alternative design elements can also be elaborated.

The attributes of the design elements are reworked until all system functions can be fulfilled without contradictions.

Developing Detailed Design

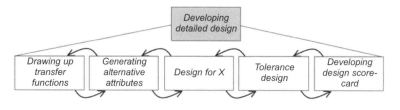

Dimensions of Developing Detailed Design

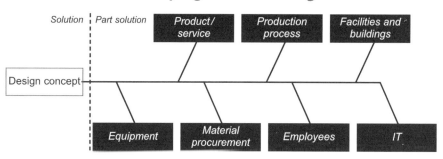

DEFINE

MEASURE

ANALYZE

DESIGN

VERIFY

Drawing up Transfer Functions

Term / Description
Transfer Function, describing the connection $y = f(x)$

When
In the Design Phase, developing detailed design

Goals
- Describe the ideal functions with the aid of a physical-mathematical model
- Evaluate the corresponding control parameters and / or design parameters

Steps

In order to specify the basic concept until the smallest detail, the transfer functions are to be considered first.

This occurs in five steps:

Iterative Process

1. **Identify**
   Apply the House of Quality and / or zigzag diagram.
2. **Decouple**
   Remove, optimize, replace or add influencing variables.
3. **Detail**
   Detail the cause and effect connection, preferably through a physical-mathe-matical analysis, after the decoupling phase. Detailing relates to the assumed connections and the sensitivity of the influencing variables.
4. **Optimize**
   After detailing the remaining dependent variables (X_{BDP}, X_{DDP}) are optimized in terms of location and spread.

   This can occur through adjustments and changes to their independent vari-ables ($X_{i\text{-}BDP}$, $X_{i\text{-}DDP}$, X_{PV}). At this point the Taguchi approach has priority: the influence of confounding variables and noise must be minimized and / or elimi-nated.
5. **Validate**
   Review the detailed design vis-à-vis CTQs and CTBs.

DEFINE

Whereas in Analyze the functions and basic design parameters are set which guarantee that the specifications are fulfilled, in the Design Phase the detailed design parameters and process variables are sought which fulfill the system functions determined in Analyze.

$$X_{BDP} = f(X_{i\text{-}DDP}, X_{DDP}) \text{ and/or } X_{DDP} = f(X_i, X_{PV})$$

In other words, the following question arises here:
Which detailed design parameters fulfill the demands of the product functions?

Transfer Functions

MEASURE

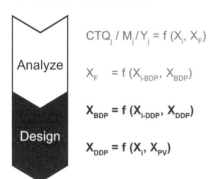

$$CTQ_j / M_j / Y_j = f(X_i, X_F)$$

$$X_F = f(X_{i\text{-}BDP}, X_{BDP})$$

$$\mathbf{X_{BDP} = f(X_{i\text{-}DDP}, X_{DDP})}$$

$$\mathbf{X_{DDP} = f(X_i, X_{PV})}$$

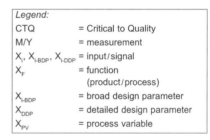

Legend:

CTQ	= Critical to Quality
M/Y	= measurement
X_i, $X_{i\text{-}BDP}$, $X_{i\text{-}DDP}$	= input/signal
X_F	= function (product/process)
$X_{i\text{-}BDP}$	= broad design parameter
X_{DDP}	= detailed design parameter
X_{PV}	= process variable

ANALYZE

The ideal function shows precisely the connection between input/signal (energy, information, material) and output (functions).

DESIGN

VERIFY

DEFINE

MEASURE

ANALYZE

DESIGN

VERIFY

Zigzag Diagram

📁 **Term / Description**
Zigzag Diagram

🕐 **When**
In the Analyze and Design Phases, developing detailed design

◎ **Goal**
Graphical illustration of the connection between design elements and system functions

▸▸ **Steps**
Arrows are used to assign the design elements to the respective product functions.

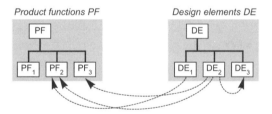

Zigzag Diagram
Example: passenger seat

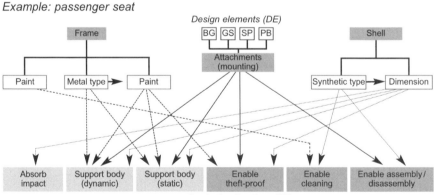

242

QFD 3

📁 **Term / Description**
Quality Function Deployment 3, QFD 3

🕐 **When**
In the Design Phase, developing detailed design

◎ **Goal**
Identify and prioritize the necessary design elements

▶▶ **Steps**
The design elements are derived, evaluated in terms of their relation to the prioritized system functions and then prioritized themselves.

QFD 3

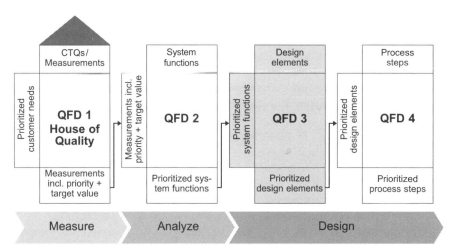

⇨ **Tip**
The QFD can be used to show possible transfer functions; it can also be used to summarize the transfer function and depict it in a clear way.

DEFINE

MEASURE

ANALYZE

DESIGN

VERIFY

Generating Alternative Characteristics of Design Elements

☐ Term/Description
Alternative options, alternative design elements

⊙ When
In the Analyze and Design Phases, developing detailed design

◎ Goal
Develop alternative design elements to optimize the sub-functions

▶▶ Steps
A variety of different analytical methods may be used to optimize the identified cause-effect relation through the targeted development of design elements.

1. *Creativity techniques*
   Zigzag diagrams, brainstorming, brain writing, mind mapping, Ishikawa, morphological box, SCAMPER, benchmarking, TRIZ

2. *Documented existing know-how*
   Mathematical, physical connections

3. *Mathematically formulated models, incl. derivatives and elasticity*
   These examine to what extent the dependent variable changes when the independent variables are modified

4. *Design of Experiments*
   Design of Experiments is another way of examining the sensitivity of systems. The data for the statistical analysis can be generated through Monte Carlo simulations, CAD-CAM (computer-aided design/manufacturing) or other simulation methods.

5. *Further statistical tools*
   Through data analysis, (e.g. hypothesis tests, ANOVA, regression) further connections can be recognized.

6. *Quality Function Deployment*
   Applying QFD matrixes structures and visualizes the connections, correlations and interdependencies between different transfer functions.

⇨ **Tip**
Disturbance variables also influence the cause-effect relation because they can lead to deviations (noise) from the ideal function. They can be identified with the help of FMEA and must be taken into consideration.

DEFINE

MEASURE

ANALYZE

DESIGN

VERIFY

DEFINE

MEASURE

ANALYZE

DESIGN

VERIFY

Tolerance Design

📁 **Term/Description**

Tolerance Design, tolerancing

🕐 **When**

In the Design Phase, developing detailed design

◎ **Goal**

Derive corresponding tolerances for the design elements

▶▶ **Steps**

Deviations were already noticeable when determining the measurements and specifications; now these are to be verified on the basis of precisely detailed transfer functions.

Setting Tolerances

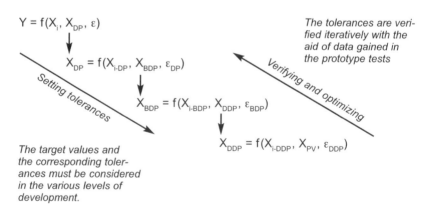

$Y = f(X_i, X_{DP}, \varepsilon)$

Setting tolerances

$X_{DP} = f(X_{i\text{-}DP}, X_{BDP}, \varepsilon_{DP})$

$X_{BDP} = f(X_{i\text{-}BDP}, X_{DDP}, \varepsilon_{BDP})$

$X_{DDP} = f(X_{i\text{-}DDP}, X_{PV}, \varepsilon_{DDP})$

The tolerances are verified iteratively with the aid of data gained in the prototype tests

Verifying and optimizing

The target values and the corresponding tolerances must be considered in the various levels of development.

Legend:
Y	= output	$X_{i\text{-}BDP}$ =	input/signal for the broad design parameter
X_i	= input/signal for the output	X_{DDP} =	detailed design parameter
X_{DP}	= design parameter	$X_{i\text{-}DDP}$ =	input/signal for the detailed design parameter
$X_{i\text{-}DP}$	= input/signal for the design parameter	X_{PV} =	process variable
X_{BDP}	= broad design parameter	ε	= noise, disturbing variables

Three different methods have proven worthwhile for such a tolerance design:

1. **Worst Case Analysis (WCA)**,
   Based on the principle: "The aggregate of the single tolerances results in the tolerance of Y."
   This method is applied to linear transfer functions. While considering all the specifications of Y, the tolerances of detailed design elements and process variables are set.

2. **Root Sum Square Method (RSS)**,
   Based on the principle: "The variation of Y is the root of the sum of single variations."
   The RSS method is also applied only to linear transfer functions. Unlike the WCA method, the variation of design elements and / or process steps are considered.

3. **Monte Carlo Analysis (MCA)**
   The Monte Carlo Analysis can also be applied to non-linear transfer functions. With the aid of special software like Crystal Ball® and Sigma Flow® distribution assumptions are made which allow conclusions to be drawn about the variation of Y. In an iterative process the single tolerances are given optimal settings.

Design for X

▢ Term/Description
Design for X, DFMA, DFC, DFR, DFS, DFE

◷ When
In the Design Phase, developing detailed design

◎ Goal
Develop reliable, cost-effective, environmentally friendly design elements

▶▶ Steps
With Design for X the entirety of the CTQs and CTBs are to flow into the product design as extensively as possible. The design considers the following aspects:

1. **Design for Manufacturing and Assembly (DFMA)**
   This method of "Design for X" is used to improve the product from the perspective of manufacturing and assembly selectively. The primary goal is to reduce the number of parts of a product as much as possible. The alternative solutions are then evaluated in terms of costs and failure resistance.

2. **Design for Configuration (DFC)**
   Design for Configuration is used to realize the required external variant diversity with a number of components and processes which is as low as possible. The interfaces and dependencies between the components are defined and their compliance with customer wishes is examined.

3. **Design for Reliability (DFR)**
   Design for Reliability anticipates failure opportunities and improves the reliability of the design. Besides reducing complexity, this is achieved by standardizing the parts and materials. The design elements should withstand or counter environment influences. Weak points which could lead to damage in packaging, transport and repairs are also to be considered.

DEFINE

MEASURE

ANALYZE

DESIGN

VERIFY

4. Design for Services (DFS)

Design for Services is applied to determine and optimize future service tasks, raise customer satisfaction, reduce life cycle costs, and improve the life span that is environmentally compatible and sustainable.

A consistent Design for Services ensures that parts are easily identifiable and accessible and the employment of modular systems reduces service demand.

The following steps are recommended for realizing a Design for Services:

1. Define the service measures
2. Simplify the diagnosis
3. Evaluate and optimize the costs for parts
4. Set and optimize the working costs
5. Simplify the entire execution

5. Design for Environment (DFE)

Design for environment looks at the ecological and economic consequences at the end of a product life cycle. It helps to reduce the environmental burden, boosts recyclability and thus reduces waste disposal costs.

The following steps reduce the impact of the product on the environment and the resulting follow-up costs:

1. Define the environmentally harmful materials / procedures
2. Define the consumption
3. Evaluate the costs (protection measures for employees and environment, disposal and consumption)
4. Search for alternative materials / procedures

Design for X
Example: passenger seat

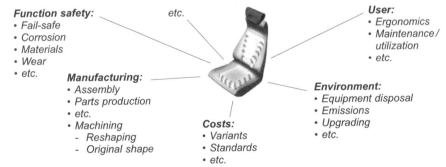

Function safety:
• Fail-safe
• Corrosion
• Materials
• Wear
• etc.

etc.

User:
• Ergonomics
• Maintenance / utilization
• etc.

Manufacturing:
• Assembly
• Parts production
• etc.
• Machining
  - Reshaping
  - Original shape

Costs:
• Variants
• Standards
• etc.

Environment:
• Equipment disposal
• Emissions
• Upgrading
• etc.

DEFINE

MEASURE

ANALYZE

DESIGN

VERIFY

Developing a Design Scorecard for the Detailed Design

📁 **Term / Description**
Design scorecard

🕓 **When**
In the Measure, Analyze and Design Phases, developing, testing and optimizing detailed design

◎ **Goal**
Document specifications and target values

▶▶ **Steps**
Once the best design elements and their specifications are set, their measurements, specifications and target values are documented in a design scorecard.
A design scorecard is formulated for each hierarchy level.

A data collection plan is drawn up to generate a baseline (sample strategy, sample size, responsibilities).

The causes for variation can be identified when validating the measurement system with Gage R&R and graphical tools depicting the results (Run Charts and Control Charts).

When formulating a design scorecard the alternative design elements are defined and can now be tested and compared.

⇨ **Tip**
The specifications of alternative design elements should be recorded in the design scorecard. Subsequent tests for selecting a best design element should use the information recorded in the design scorecard as a valid basis.

Design Scorecards on Different Hierarchy Levels

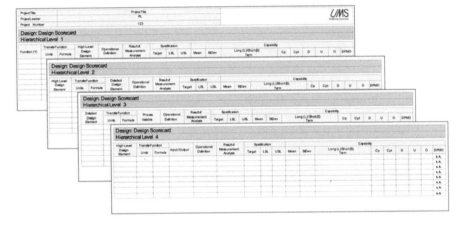

DEFINE

MEASURE

ANALYZE

DESIGN

VERIFY

Testing Detailed Design

📁 **Term / Description**

Testing Detailed System Design

🕐 **When**

In the Design Phase, testing detailed design

◎ **Goal**

Test all alternative elements of the developed detailed design

⏩ **Steps**

- The selected design elements are implemented physically or virtually in a prototype. Alternative characteristics are compared with the aid of statistical methods.
- The best detailed design is selected on the basis of set criteria.
- The corresponding design scorecards are adjusted if necessary.
- These steps can occur iteratively.

Testing Detailed Design

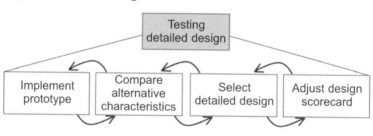

252

Implementing Prototype

📋 **Term / Description**
Prototyping, implementing prototype

🕐 **When**
In the Analyze and Design Phases, testing detailed design

◎ **Goals**
- Identify the best alternatives
- Identify the risks in the selected detailed design
- Derive suitable improvement measures

▶▶ **Steps**
A prototype can be realized in a physical or a simulated model setup of the system to be developed:

1. **Traditional method (tool and die)**
   Here the product is realized physically. The tool-and-die method is often applied to analyze the peculiarities of repairs and maintenance (e.g. construct a break system to test wear and maintenance work).

2. **Rapid method (CAD method):**
   The further development of computer applications means that the CAD method (Computer-Aided Design) is increasingly preferred to the tool-and-die approach. The products and their transfer functions can be depicted more and more realistically. In contrast to tool-and-die, CAD is more cost-effective and timesaving.

DEFINE

MEASURE

ANALYZE

DESIGN

VERIFY

Comparing Alternative Design

🗀 Term/Description
Alternative Design Comparison

🕐 When
In the Analyze and Design Phases, testing detailed design

◎ Goals
- Compare the performance capability of alternative design characteristics
- Optimize the detailed design

▶▶ Steps
Depending on the problem and the data type, different statistical tools can be used to compare the alternative characteristics.

Use of different statistical tools according to the data type

		Output (Y)	
		Continuous	*Discrete*
Input (X)	*Continuous*	• Correlation • Simple and multiple linear regression • Non-linear regression • DOE	• Logistic regression • DOE
	Discrete	• Tests for mean value • Tests for variances • Non-parametric tests • Variance analysis • DOE	• Tests for proportion (one and two proportion test, χ^2-test) • DOE

254

Hypothesis Testing

📋 Term / Description
Hypothesis Testing, Significance Tests

🕐 When
In the Analyze and Design Phases, testing detailed design

◎ Goals
– Data-based comparison of different concepts
– Determine the influencing factors

▶▶ Steps
When working with data from design projects inferences on the relations in the population should be drawn from a low number of samples.
It is therefore first necessary to identify the scope a sample must have to enable a valid statement about the true parameters (e.g. mean value, median, proportions, variance, etc.) of the population.

Population and Sample

Population

Sample

Confidence intervals are formed to compare the parameters calculated from the samples with equivalents from the population. The confidence intervals assert that with a confidence level which is determined by the

255

DEFINE

MEASURE

ANALYZE

DESIGN

VERIFY

testing person in advance set beforehand (usually 95% and/or 99% or a significance level of 5% and/or 1%), the true values (parameters) from the population lie within these intervals.

Confidence interval for mean value

$$\left[\bar{x} - z\left[\frac{s}{\sqrt{n}}\right]; \bar{x} + z\left[\frac{s}{\sqrt{n}}\right]\right]$$

The breadth of the confidence interval is influenced by the spread of the sample (s), the certainty (z), and the sample size (n). The sample size n is determined in turn by the temporal effort and the resulting costs for the examination, but also depends on the desired meaningfulness of the values which are to be generated.

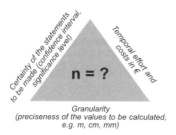

Granularity
(preciseness of the values to be calculated,
e.g. m, cm, mm)

In general using rules of thumb suffices for calculating the suitable sample size.

Sample size for continuous data

$$n = \left\lceil\left(\frac{z \cdot s}{\Delta}\right)^2\right\rceil$$

n = sample size
z = this value is taken from a chart; it depends on the selected confidence interval. Here $z_{95\%} = 1.96$ and/or $z_{99\%} = 2.575$
s = standard deviation of the sample
Δ = granularity (preciseness of the calculated values in the unit of s, e.g. m, cm, mm)
⌈x⌉ = this symbol means that the number x is rounded up to the next whole number

256

DEFINE

Sample size for discrete data

$$n = \left\lceil \left(\frac{z}{\Delta}\right)^2 \hat{p} \cdot (1 - \hat{p}) \right\rceil$$

n = sample size

z = this value is taken from a chart; it depends on the selected confidence interval. Here $z_{95\%}$ = 1.96 or $z_{99\%}$ = 2.575

$\hat{p}$ = proportion of defective units in the sample, e.g. 32% defective units correspond to p = 0.32. If the proportion p is unknown, then it is initially calculated with p = 0.5.

Δ = granularity (preciseness of the calculated values in the unit of p, e.g. 10% = 0.1, 1% = 0.01, etc.)

$\lceil x \rceil$ = this symbol means that the number x is rounded up to the next whole number

Side condition: $n \cdot p \geq 5$ or $n \cdot (1 - p) \geq 5$

Hypothesis tests can be carried out on the basis of the taken samples to compare concepts or determine the influencing factors.

A statistical test is a procedure that uses a test statistic to verify the statistical validity (significance) of a hypothesis for a sample.

Such a hypothesis test is based on the formulation of two complimentary assertions: the null hypothesis H_0 and the alternative hypothesis H_A.

MEASURE

– The **null hypothesis H_0** asserts:
There is equality; there's no difference!

– The **alternative hypothesis H_A** asserts:
There is no equality; there is a difference!

ANALYZE

Statistical tests can only ascertain differences, not accordances. For this reason, as a rule the null hypothesis is established in order to be refuted.

Making decisions on the basis of statistical tests entails a certain degree of uncertainty: one cannot be 100% certain that the decision is correct. At the same time, however, statistical tests are designed in such a way that the probability of making an incorrect decision is minimized.

DESIGN

A null hypothesis is rejected when the result of a sample shows that the validity of the established null hypothesis is improbable. What is ultimately

VERIFY

DEFINE

MEASURE

ANALYZE

DESIGN

VERIFY

considered to be improbable is determined in advance by the so-called significance level and/or confidence interval. The most frequently used significance levels are 0.05 (= 5%) and 0.01 (= 1%), and/or 95% and 99% confidence intervals. The significance level is connected with the potential wrong decisions.

There are basically two types of wrong decisions or errors in statistical tests: the α-error and the β-error.

The α- and the β-error

Decision		Reality	
		H_0	H_A
	H_0	Correct decision	Error of the second type (β-error)
	H_A	Error of the first type (α-error)	Correct decision

The null hypothesis is not rejected although it is not valid in reality.
A difference in the population is not identified.

The null hypothesis is rejected although it is valid in reality.

The statistical decision is made by comparing the significance level (α) with the p-value (p = probability). The p-value indicates the actual probability from the present samples that the null hypothesis is falsely rejected. The p-value thus matches the residual risk when rejecting the null hypothesis. For this reason it is also known as the error probability. The p-value is calculated with statistics software like Minitab®.

– If the p-value is small, e.g. smaller than the set α (significance level), the null hypothesis must be rejected. The following phrase sums up what is to be done: "If p is low, H_0 must go!"

– If the p-value is larger than the α-level, this means that possibly emerging differences are not statistically significant.

A statistical test occurs in the following steps:
1. Define the problem and goal (what is to be investigated for which purpose?)
2. Formulate the hypotheses (H_0: condition of equality)
3. Set the significance level α (as a rule $\alpha = 0.05$ or $\alpha = 0.01$)
4. Select suitable statistical test (e.g. two-sample t-test)
5. Carry out the test statistic with the aid of a program (e.g. Minitab®)
6. Interpret the test statistic and/or p-value
7. Make your decision
8. Verify your decision. If H_0 is not rejected, then verify β with the aid of a statistics program!

There are a great number of statistical hypothesis tests. Some practice-relevant tests are described on the following pages.

Discrete Data – testing proportions

Test	When / What for	Hypotheses	Prerequisites
Binomial Test One Proportion Test	Compare a proportion with a theoretical or given proportion with binominally distributed data, e.g.: good (non-defective)/bad (defective) test.	$H_0: p = p_{Target}$ $H_A: p \neq p_{Target}$	Binominally distributed data $n \geq 100$ and/or $n \cdot p \geq 5$ and $n \cdot (1-p) \geq 5$
Binomial Test Two Proportion Test	Compare proportions of a characteristic in two samples.	$H_0: p_1 = p_2$ $H_A: p_1 \neq p_2$	Binominally distributed data $n \geq 100$ and/or $n \cdot p \geq 5$ and $n \cdot (1-p) \geq 5$
χ^2 (homogeneity) Test Chi-Square Test	1. Compare proportions of a characteristic in two or more samples. 2. Compare proportions in two or more populations.	$H_0: p_1^1 = p_1^2 = \ldots = p_1^j$ $p_2^1 = p_2^2 = \ldots = p_2^j$ $\vdots$ $p_j^1 = p_j^2 = \ldots = p_j^j$ $H_A:$ *at least one proportion is different.*	Nominal data $n \geq 100$ and/or $n \cdot p \geq 5$ and $n \cdot (1-p) \geq 5$

DEFINE

MEASURE

ANALYZE

DESIGN

VERIFY

Continuous Data – testing the mean value

Test	When/What for	Hypotheses	Prerequisites
One Sample t Test	Compare the mean value of a sample with a target value	$H_0 : \mu = \mu_{Target}$ $H_A : \mu \neq \mu_{Target}$	$n \geq 30$ and/or normally distributed data
Two Sample t Test	Compare mean values of two independent samples	$H_0 : \mu_1 = \mu_2$ $H_A : \mu_1 \neq \mu_2$	$n \geq 30$ and/or normally distributed data, independent samples
Two Sample paired t Test	Compare mean values of two dependent samples	$H_0 : \mu_1 = \mu_2$ $H_A : \mu_1 \neq \mu_2$	$n \geq 30$ and/or normally distributed data, paired, dependent samples
One Way ANOVA	Compare mean values of several independent samples	$H_0 : \mu_1 = \mu_2 = ... = \mu_i$ $H_A :$ *at least one mean value is different.*	Equal variances or equal samples, independent samples

DEFINE

MEASURE

ANALYZE

DESIGN

VERIFY

Continuous Data – testing variances

Test	When/What for	Hypotheses	Prerequisites
F-Test / Levene's Test Two Variances	Compare variances of two independent samples	$H_0 : \sigma_1^2 = \sigma_2^2$ $H_A : \sigma_1^2 \neq \sigma_2^2$	F-Test: normally distributed data. Levene's Test: no distribution assumption, independent samples
Bartlett's / Levene's Test) Test For Equal Variances	Compare variances of several independent samples	$H_0 : \sigma_1^2 = \sigma_2^2 = ... = \sigma_i^2$ H_A: at least one variance is different	Bartlett's Test: normally distributed data. Levene's Test: no distribution assumption, independent samples

One Sample t Test

```
One Sample T: Paint Thickness

Test of mu = 140 vs not = 140


Variable    N    Mean    StDev  SE Mean            95% CI     T      P
Paint
thickness  80  153,859  35,654   3,986  (145,925; 161,793)  3,48  0,001
```

Result:
Here p is < 0.05. There is a statistically significant difference. The hypothesis H_0 can be rejected.

DEFINE

One Sample t Test

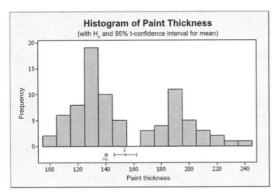

Graphic result:
the difference between
the target and mean values
of the sample is statistically
significant.
The hypothesis H_0 can be
rejected.

MEASURE

ANALYZE

DESIGN

VERIFY

263

Design of Experiments (DOE)

📁 **Term / Description**

Design of Experiments, DOE

🕒 **When**

In the Analyze and Design Phases, testing detailed design, optimizing the lean process

◎ **Goals**

- Data-based comparison of different concepts
- Determine the significant factors, their effects and interactions
- Draw up and / or compliment the transfer functions
- Determine the optimal characteristics (design parameters)
- Determine the optimal equipment settings (process variables)

▶▶ **Steps**

1. Define the optimization task and set the response
2. Identify the influencing variables
3. Determine the relevant factor levels
4. Derive the experiment strategy: set the suitable design and sample size
5. Ensure the measurement capability
6. Conduct experiments and collect data
7. Analyze the results and derive measures

1. Define the optimization tasks and set the responses

- Select the product or process to be analyzed
- Set the goals
- Set the responses for measuring whether the goals are achieved
- Make sure that the responses have the following characteristics:
  - *Completeness:* all key process and product characteristics were covered
  - *Dissimilarity:* each response describes a different relation
  - *Relevance:* each response bears a clear relation to the goal of the analysis

- *Linearity:* if there are several similar responses, select the one that depends linearly on the influencing variables
- *Quantification:* the responses should be as continuous and / or metric as possible

2. Identify the influencing variables

- Locate and hold the decisive influencing variables with the aid of structured brainstorming. The most important tools are:
  - Cause-and-effect diagram
  - Tool 3 (testing the relation between output and input measurements and process measurements)
  - FMEA
- Results gained in the process and data analysis can also be taken into account:
  - Data stratification
  - Hypothesis tests
  - Variance analysis
  - Regression analysis
- The final evaluation should be based on the following criteria:
  - Importance of a factor
  - Accuracy of the possible setting
  - Reproducibility of the setting
  - Effort and expense for changing the levels

3. Determine the relevant factor levels

- A maximum and minimum are set as factor levels.
  Two factor levels are selected initially:
  - Continuous influencing variables: the maximum and minimum should lie in a sensible area so that the response is still quantifiable
  - Discrete influencing factors: if the factor levels are discrete, e.g. there are five producers, one refers initially to the two most important factor levels

4. Derive the experiment strategy

- Set the sample sizes (plan the experiment scope)
- Determine the number of blocks
- Decide on randomization or take into consideration restrictions in randomization (e.g. due to the costs of the experiment setup)

DEFINE

MEASURE

ANALYZE

DESIGN

VERIFY

– Determine the factor level combinations: full-factorial or fractional factorial DOE

Full-factorial DOE
- All factor settings are combined in a full-factorial DOE.

Full-Factorial DOE
Example: fuel consumption

Speed (km/h)	Tire pressure (Bar)	Fuel (Octane)	Consumption (l/100km)
100	2	91	10
150	2	91	15
100	3	91	9
150	3	91	7
100	2	98	9
150	2	98	14
100	3	98	6.5
150	3	98	13

- In this way, the effects generated by the factors and their interactions can be identified completely.
- The amount of characteristic combinations to be examined depends exponentially on the number of factors:

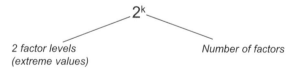

$$2^k$$

2 factor levels (extreme values)   Number of factors

Fractional factorial DOE
- Fractional factorial DOEs (or part-factorial) reduce the number of single tests.

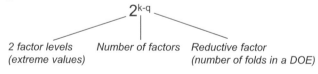

$$2^{k-q}$$

2 factor levels (extreme values)   Number of factors   Reductive factor (number of folds in a DOE)

- Testing the significance of the factors is still possible because the loss of information refers to the confounding of specific effects, e.g. the effects of main factors and interactions are indistinguishable from one another. Which kind of confounding is present depends on the corresponding resolution type.

Resolution types of fractional factorial DOE

		Number of factors												
Number of experiments		2	3	4	5	6	7	8	9	10	11	12	13	14	15
	4	Full	III												
	8		Full	IV	III	III	III								
	16			Full	V	IV	IV	IV	III	III	III	III	III	III	III
	32				Full	VI	IV	IV	IV	IV	IV	IV	IV	IV	IV
	64					Full	VII	V	IV	IV	IV	IV	IV	IV	IV
	128						Full	VIII	VI	V	V	IV	IV	IV	IV

Resolution type	Confounding	Evaluation
III	Main factors are confounded with two-factor interaction	Critical
IV	Main factors with three-factor interaction / two-factor interaction with two-factor interaction	Less critical
V	Main factors with four-factor interaction / two-factor interaction with three-factor interaction	Uncritical

The analysis occurs the same way as in a full-factorial design.

DEFINE

MEASURE

ANALYZE

DESIGN

VERIFY

DEFINE

MEASURE

ANALYZE

DESIGN

VERIFY

– As a rule, a full-factorial DOE is too expensive and elaborate. The following procedure is recommended (block procedure) if the experiments can be conducted successively:

- *Block 0: Good-Bad Trials*
    • There are 2 different settings for each factor which lead to distinctly different values of the observed responses. All of the factors are set so that a "good" result can be expected (e.g. low defect rates, high levels of agent concentration) according to expert opinion. Next, all of the factors are set so that a "bad" result can be expected (e.g. high defect rate, low concentration of agents).
    • The goal is to ascertain whether there are any effects at all. If no effects are located this can be due to the fact that the selected factors are not relevant or the signal-noise relationship is too weak, i.e. the noise is too "loud". At this point the experiments should be stopped and, if required, further factors should be determined or the noise should be eliminated.

- *Block 1: Screening Experiments*
    • It is not unusual that 10 or even up to 15 factors are selected.
    • If effects exist in principle experiments with resolution III or IV should be carried out first.
    • The important question here is: are there effects of a sufficient dimension?
    • The goal is to locate the relevant factors in this phase ("separate the wheat from the chaff"). It is often possible to significantly reduce the number of relevant factors and conduct further DOEs based on far fewer experiments.
    • When deciding to leave out factors attention needs to be paid to possible interactions. In practice we therefore avoid reducing factors in a resolution III.

- *Block 2: Fold-Over Experiments*
    Fold-over experiments supplement screening DOEs, i.e. supplement action by the missing experiments to achieve a better resolution type.
    This is a reversal of the signs deployed in the starting DOE.
    • The goal is to reduce the number of factors to the really important ones. This makes it possible to estimate the interactions.

DEFINE

- • The statistical analysis can provide the beginnings for the optimal settings (Response Optimizer).

- *Block 3: Completion Experiments*
  - • If there is reason to assume that the relationships are non-linear, i.e. squared effects exist or effects of a higher order, additional experiments are carried out which, besides the minimum and maximum settings, take into consideration additional mean values.
  - • This is known as the Response Surface Methodology (Central Composite Design).

- *Block 4: Optimization Experiments*
  - • Optimal settings are proposed when analyzing the statistics generated by the preceding experiments.
  - • The goal now is to test the optimal settings of the factors.

MEASURE

Estimate the costs: make sure that the costs are reasonable in relation to the hoped-for results. If the expense appears to be too great, then examine whether the costs can be reduced by doing without factors and factor levels, by block building or randomization, or carrying out a smaller number of experiments – without, of course, endangering the goal. If this proves unfeasible, the goal should be reconsidered.

ANALYZE

5. Ensure the measurement system capability
- – Develop the Operational Definition and carry out a Measurement System Analysis.
- – A Measurement System Analysis verifies if the measurement system is suitable. Improve the system whenever required.

DESIGN

6. Conduct experiments and collect data
- – Prior to actually conducting the experiments it is recommended to carry out a couple of preliminary tests or pilots. The goal is to see whether the estimated expense and effort is realistic, and if the result is consistent, i.e. the noise has been eliminated.
- – When conducting the experiments make sure that everything runs according to plan. This means that each of the experiments has to be monitored individually.

VERIFY

7. Analyze the results and derive measures

- The statistical analysis of the results proceeds according to the methodologies of the regression (smallest square method) and variance analyses.
- The graphic and analytical results are reviewed after each block so as to determine the next steps. In this respect, carrying out DOE is an iterative process.
- When analyzing the results and deciding on the next steps, one or several experts involved in the process should always be consulted so as to avoid drawing misleading conclusions. Such conclusions can conceal the true relationships, e.g. through measurement errors or noise. The results need to be checked at all times to see if they make sense.

⇨ **Tips**

- Along with the mean values as responses, a classical factorial DOE is also suitable for observing the variance. In this case the factors responsible for the variation can be recognized and a meaningful reduction of variation can be undertaken.
- To stabilize variation it is necessary to transform the variance s^2. This is done either through the root transformation (in this case the result is the standard deviation s) or a logarithmic transformation ($\ln [s^2]$).
- For considering the standard deviation as a response, several measurements of an experiment, so-called "repeats" are necessary.

270

DEFINE

MEASURE

ANALYZE

DESIGN

VERIFY

Examples of DOE applications in manufacturing

Product	Response (Y)	Factors (X)
Baking mix	• Weight 1cm^3	• Amount of flour • Amount of baking powder • Granularity of cocoa
Baking oven	• Degree of browning • Uniformity of browning	• Ventilation speed • Form of heating spiral • Sealing
Can	• Width • Depth	• Color aluminum • Amount of oil • Construction A / B • Tools H / Z

Examples of DOE applications in services

Branch	Response (Y)	Factors (X)
Logistics	• Inventory costs	• Supplier • Delivery conditions • Payment conditions
Market research	• Willingness to acquire the product (ranking scale)	• Description of product attributes • Packaging • Placement
Financial services	• Lead time for processing the request	• Processing a form (manual or electronic) • Approval • Processing (sequential or parallel) • Processor (branch special-ist or general education)

DEFINE

MEASURE

ANALYZE

DESIGN

VERIFY

Design of Experiments for the example of the passenger seat

The DFSS team must decide on a paint type for the coating of the seat frame.
– In the high-level design it was decided to use a standard alloy for the frame material.
– The CTQs of corrosion and wear resistance can only be achieved with this alloy through the paint work.
– The paint of the manufacturer Xylosud and the manufacturer Müller can be chosen. Both produce a corrosion-resistant paint which is effective in case one of the usual liquids comes into contact with the paint (cleaning agents, sulfuric acids, coke, juice).
– With the help of DOE the team decides to examine the suitability of the paint in terms of its thickness.

The question that needs to be answered is: which paint and which pretreatment achieve the greatest wear resistance.

Output measurement is:
Y1: paint thickness

Input and process measurements	**Factor levels [- ; +]**
X1 : temperature	[20; 25]
X2 : pressure	[15; 30]
X3 : thinner	[10; 20]
X4 : pretreatment	[A; B]

Determining the relevant factors and interactions is supported by a statistics program (such as Minitab®).

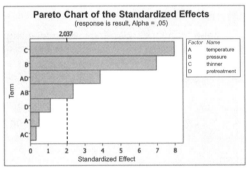

The dotted line shows a confidence level of 5%, i.e. α-value = 0.05.

272

The graphical result of the analysis is a Pareto Chart. The statistically sig-nificant factors have longer bars which pass the red line (significance level 5%).

The optimal settings can then be identified with the Response Optimizer.

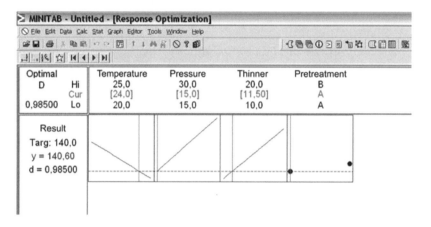

The DOE helps to identify the optimal settings for the continuous factors such as temperature, pressure and thinner as well as the best pretreatment for the paintwork.

DEFINE

MEASURE

ANALYZE

DESIGN

VERIFY

Selecting Detailed Design

☐ **Term / Description**
Select Detailed Design, Pugh Matrix

🕑 **When**
In the Analyze and Design Phases, developing, testing and optimizing detailed design

◎ **Goal**
Criteria-based selection of the best design concept

▸▸ **Step**
A criteria-based selection of different detailed designs or design elements can be carried out using a Pugh Matrix (see Analyze Phase).

Pugh Matrix

Alternative / Criteria	Detailed design 1	Detailed design 2 (Standard)	Detailed design 3	Prioritization
Criterion 1	+	0	-	3
Criterion 2	+	0	-	4
Criterion 3	0	0	+	2
Criterion 4	-	0	0	1
Aggregate +				
Aggregate -				
Aggregate 0				
Weighted aggregate +				
Weighted aggregate -				

Adjusting Design Scorecards

📁 **Term / Description**

Design scorecard

🕐 **When**

In the Analyze and Design Phases

◎ **Goals**

- Update the design scorecards with the final design parameters
- Document the final design parameters

▶▶ **Steps**

The design scorecards are adjusted, extended and finalized with the new specifications formulated in the Design Phase.

Design scorecards with different hierarchy levels

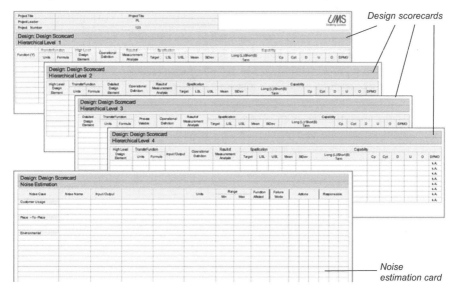

Design scorecards

Noise estimation card

DEFINE

MEASURE

ANALYZE

DESIGN

VERIFY

Risk Evaluation

📁 **Term/Description**
Risk Evaluation, analysis of the detailed product design, analysis of weak points in the detailed design concept

🕐 **When**
In the Analyze and Design Phases, optimizing detailed design

◎ **Goals**
– Locate potential failures
– Derive counter measures

▶▶ **Steps**
Prior to beginning with process development it is important to systematically evaluate the detailed product/process design with respect to possible weak points.
For this purpose the following questions must be answered:
– Is it possible for design elements to be forgotten, mistaken or falsely assembled?
– Would an increased production effort be required?
– Do auxiliary tools or special gadgets have to be built?
– What types of burden on the system are possible?
– What happens in case of incorrect handling?

There are a number of methods for examining possible weak points in a selected detailed design:
– Anticipatory Failure Detection *(see Analyze)*
– FMEA *(see Analyze)*
– Poka Yoke

Avoiding Risks

📁 **Term / Description**
Poka Yoke, avoiding defects and risks

🕒 **When**
In the Design Phase, optimizing detailed design

◎ **Goal**
Take measures to ensure elimination of errors by 100%

▶▶ **Steps**
Potential errors are analyzed and prevented before they can occur by corresponding measures.

There are a number of different error types:
- **Operating error:** twisting, changing or mistaking parts
- **Forgetfulness:** important working steps are forgotten
- **Misunderstandings:** people see alleged solutions before they are familiar with the situation
- **Overlooking:** errors occur because people do not look at an object long enough or close enough
- **Beginners:** errors due to lacking experience
- **Inadvertent error:** errors due to lacking attention
- **Slowness:** errors when workflows are unexpectedly stopped and / or slowed down
- **Lacking standards:** errors due to missing and / or incomplete working or process descriptions
- **Surprises:** errors when workflows run different than expected
- **Willful error:** errors due to consciously ignoring rules and regulations
- **Intentional error:** errors made deliberately, e.g. sabotage or theft

The following steps are taken to prevent (Yoke, Japanese for "preventing") these errors (Poka, Japanese for "error"):

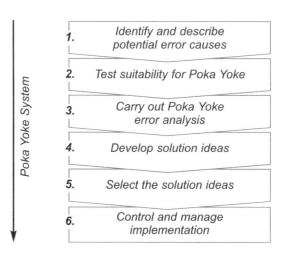

Poka Yoke System

1. Identify and describe potential error causes

2. Test suitability for Poka Yoke

3. Carry out Poka Yoke error analysis

4. Develop solution ideas

5. Select the solution ideas

6. Control and manage implementation

1. Identify and describe potential error causes

The error-relevant data is analyzed from different perspectives:
- Location and frequency of error pattern
- Type of error (stochastic or systematic)
- Point of time when the error was detected
- Significance and impact of the error

The goal is a detailed and measurable description of the error pattern and the error environment

2. Test suitability for Poka Yoke

In the Poka Yoke system a sufficient specification of the error pattern is a prerequisite for a successful error elimination.

The following questions should thus be answered with yes:
- Is the point of origin of the error pattern known?
- Is the part causing the error known?
- Is the activity causing the error known?

If more than one question is answered with no, then the error must be further specified:

278

3. Carry out Poka Yoke error analysis

An analysis of the error and the process in which it originates occurs by:
- Observing the error and its causes
- Reviewing the SOPs and possible deviations from the standard procedure
- Determining the Poka Yoke error type (see above)
- Observing the effects of the error

4. Develop solution ideas

On the basis of the error analysis the team elaborates at least three alternative ideas for solutions.
Remarks on feasibility and potential of these ideas can already be noted down at this point.

5. Select the solution ideas

With the aid of a Pugh Matrix the solution alternatives are evaluated and prioritized in terms of the following aspects:
- Feasibility / implementation
- Costs / benefits
- Potential for avoiding errors
- Effects on the process and / or follow-up process

In this way the best Poka Yoke solution can be identified. If no solutions for preventing errors can be identified at the origin, then the error needs to be detected as early as possible.
See examination methods on the following page.

6. Control and manage implementation

To ensure a stable implementation of the selected Poka Yoke solution the following activities should be carried out:
- Plan and document resources and activities required for implementation
- Initiate, accompany and monitor implementation
- Define reaction plans
- Control the error pattern and if required take counter measures (PDCA)

279

DEFINE

MEASURE

ANALYZE

DESIGN

VERIFY

Examination Methods

Examination methods		
Traditional examination		• Discerns good parts and scrap / rework • Reduces the defective parts delivered to the customers • Does not prevent error production • Slows feedback via scrap / rework
Statistical examination		• System for reducing examination costs • Does not prevent error production, does not ensure non-defective parts • Errors can be passed through due to examination of samples • Slows feedback via scrap / rework
Continuous examination		• Every process step examines the quality of the previous process • 100% of the parts are examined • Does not prevent error production • High effort / expenses of examination – efficient only for small amounts
Self-examination		• Every process step examines its own quality • Immediate feedback and corrective measures • Stops the further processing of a defective part • High effort / expenses of examination – 100% of the parts are examined
Complete examination		• Every process examine its own quality and that of its supplier • Problems are identified before the process step is finished • Immediate feedback and corrective measures • Stops the further processing of a defective part • High effort / expenses of examination – 100% of the parts are examined

Poka Yoke
Examples

Error prevention:
Using clearly dimensioned locking systems directly prevents errors.

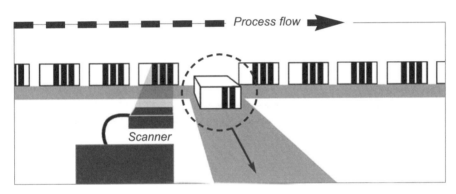

Defective units are ejected

Early identification of errors
A barcode system identifies defective units.

DEFINE

MEASURE

ANALYZE

DESIGN

VERIFY

Reviewing the Performance Capability for the Target Production

☐ Term / Description
Performance Analysis for Future State Production, examination and evaluation of the current performance capability for the target production

◷ When
In the Design Phase, reviewing performance capability for the target production

◎ Goal
Decide on the usability of existing process and input variables

▶▶ Steps
- Identify necessary process variables
- Review the current performance capability of the target production

QFD 4

🗀 Term/Description
Quality Function Deployment 4, QFD 4, House of Quality 4

🕐 When
In the Design Phase, reviewing the performance capability for the target production

◎ Goal
Identify and prioritize the necessary process steps

▸▸ Steps
The process steps are derived, evaluated according to their relation to the prioritized design elements, and are finally prioritized.

QFD 4

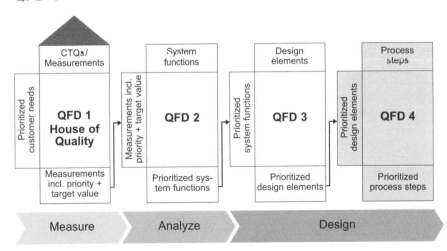

DEFINE

MEASURE

ANALYZE

DESIGN

VERIFY

Evaluating the Current Process Performance

☐ Term / Description

Evaluation of process performance / capability, evaluation of the current performance capability of the production components

⊘ When

In the Design Phase, reviewing the performance capability for the target production

◎ Goal

Decide on the usability of existing process and input variables

▶▶ Steps

All relevant dimensions have to be evaluated with respect to quality, capacity and costs.

One can distinguish between the following variables:
– Process
– Facilities and premises layout
– Equipment
– Material procurement
– Employees
– IT

Process and Input Variables

Process	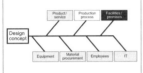	• Is the process existing today capable of producing the desired quality? • Is the existing process capable of delivering the amounts corresponding to the customer need? • Can the existing process remain within the planned production costs?
Facilities / buildings	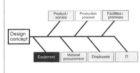	• Do the facilities match current environmental, health and safety standards? • Are the facilities capable of delivering 5S standards? • Is there enough storage area? • Is the operating concept suitable for a good production management – are the distances small?
Equipment	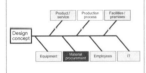	• Is the existing equipment (machines / tools) capable of delivering the desired quality? • Are the right tools available in the right amount? • Are the costs for tools and facilities affordable (operating costs, wear, etc.)?
Material procurement	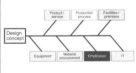	• Is the quality of the standard material sufficient? • Can the material be procured in sufficient amounts at the requested date? • Do the procurement costs of the material match the planning?
Employees		• Are the employees sufficiently trained to adequately manufacture the product? • Are enough employees available? • Are the labor costs within the planning scope?
IT		• Is IT support for the process ensured, e.g. order and inventory management, quality management? • Are all used materials recorded in the system? • Are the IT costs within the planning scope?

DEFINE

MEASURE

ANALYZE

DESIGN

VERIFY

The single evaluations should to be as quantitative as possible, based on key performance indicators or key figures (e.g. C_p, C_{pk}, costs, capacity) and control charts.

The results of the evaluation are presented systematically in a matrix. The following question is decisive for the evaluation of the evaluated production components:
To what extent are the necessary requirements of the individual components fulfilled?
An evaluation matrix visualizes the results.

Evaluation Matrix

Design element	Evaluation				
	1	2	3	4	5
Production process					
Facilities / premises layout					
Equipment					
Material procurement					
Employees					
IT					

Criteria:	Evaluation:
○ Quality	1 = is fulfilled by 0%
	2 = is fulfilled by 25%
◐ Costs	3 = is fulfilled by 50%
	4 = is fulfilled by 75%
● Capacity	5 = is fulfilled by 100%

A decision on how to proceed is to be made on the basis of this overview.

286

DEFINE

Optimization Direction on the Basis of Evaluation Results

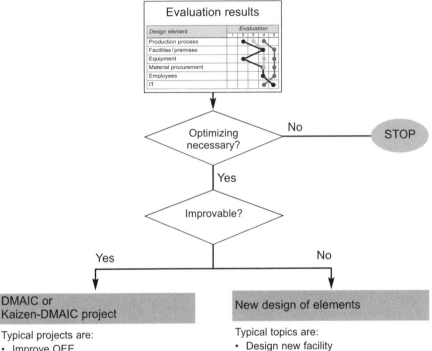

MEASURE

ANALYZE

DMAIC or Kaizen-DMAIC project

Typical projects are:
- Improve OEE
- Reduce setup times
- Optimize machine settings
- Optimize supply chains
- …

New design of elements

Typical topics are:
- Design new facility
- Redesign supply chain
- Reorganize tools
- Reorganize production layout
- …

If the prerequisites are not given for an efficient production, a new production process needs to be developed.

DESIGN

VERIFY

DEFINE

MEASURE

ANALYZE

DESIGN

VERIFY

Developing and Optimizing Lean Process

📁 **Term/Description**
Process Development

🕐 **When**
In the Design Phase, developing and optimizing the lean process

◎ **Goal**
Develop an efficient and effective process in detail

▶▶ **Steps**
1. Depict the key process steps
2. Visualize the detailed process
3. Draw up standard operating procedures and working procedures
4. Minimize process lead time
5. Plan facilities and buildings
6. Plan equipment
7. Plan material procurement
8. Ensure employees are available
9. Provide IT
10. Evaluate and optimize detailed concept

⇒ **Tips**
•   Simulations during the Design Phase support the validation and detailing of the design concept.
•   Besides the specific design of all process variables it must be ensured that the production process and product comply with external and internal requirements (pay attention to regulatory requirements!).

SIPOC

📁 **Term / Description**
SIPOC (Supplier, Input, Process, Output, Customer)

🕒 **When**
In the Analyze and Design Phases, developing lean process

◎ **Goal**
– Generate an overview of the process to be developed
– Determine the key inputs and their suppliers
– Determine the key outputs and the corresponding (internal and external) customers

▶▶ **Steps**
– Set the start and end points of the process
– Depict the process roughly (in 5-10 steps)
– Identify key inputs / suppliers and outputs / customers

SIPOC

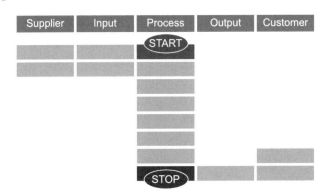

289

DEFINE

MEASURE

ANALYZE

DESIGN

VERIFY

Process Diagram

☐ Term / Description
Flow Chart, Cross Functional Diagram, Swim Lane Diagram, Process Function Diagram, PFD

☉ When
In the Design Phase, developing lean process

◎ Goals
- Visualize the process structure
- Describe the individual process steps
- Clarify the complexity (number of handovers etc.)
- Visualize responsibilities
- Reveal optimization potentials

▶▶ Steps
- Depict the process on a high level (e.g. SIPOC)
- Emphasize the start and end points
- Identify the detailed process steps and the respective persons responsible
- Depict all process steps in their actual and current position in the correct flow

Process Function Diagram

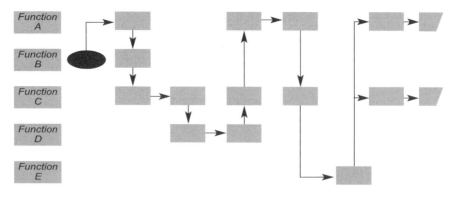

Value Stream Map

📁 **Term/Description**
Value Stream Map, VSM

🕐 **When**
In the Design Phase, developing lean process

◎ **Goals**
– Planning and transparency of the material and information flow from supplier to the end customer
– Identify sources of scrap and their causes

▶▶ **Steps**
1. Define product groups and/or product families
2. Describe the process on a high level
3. Determine detail level of the process level
4. Visualize the process
5. Determine the material and information flow
6. Add data boxes, determine the measurements to be set and collect data
7. Define and identify the times operationally

1. Define product groups and/or product families
If more than one product is produced in a plant/in a building/in a factory the focus is on a meaningful product group or family.

2. Describe the process on a high level
A process description on a low level of detail serves as the starting point for the step-by-step identification of the relevant process variables (e.g. SIPOC).

3. Determine the level of detail of the process level
A "top down" process diagram can be used to subdivide the process steps and define the relevant process levels.

DEFINE

MEASURE

ANALYZE

DESIGN

VERIFY

DEFINE

MEASURE

ANALYZE

DESIGN

VERIFY

4. Visualize the process
In order to sketch the process stream it is helpful to move upstream in the value stream and begin with the customer-relevant sub-processes (e.g. shipping). The following symbols are used in the VSM for the process flow.

Process Symbols

Process step

Customers/suppliers

Stock/amount of stock

Rework

Scrap

Visualizing the Process

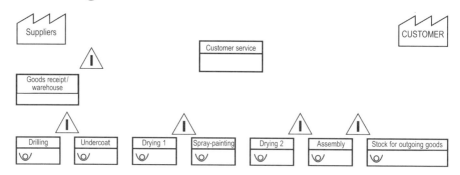

5. Determine the material and information flow
In a first step the movements taken by the materials are described as they pass between the sketched process steps in the target process. The steering principles in the production process (Pull and Push Systems) are taken into consideration.

Symbols for Material Flow

Transport　　*Push*　　*Pull*　　*Product to customer*　　*First-in-first-out sequence*

Steering Principles in the Production Process

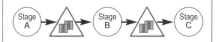

Push System: planning based

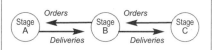

Pull System: demand-steered

A process produces without considera-tion of the actual need of the following (internal) customer process and pushes the intermediate product through the process. Production operates in line with an established production plan.

For traditional batch-size production in Push Systems "optimal" batches are calculated for production sectors operat-ing independently of one another. Each sector pushes its produced parts into a buffer for the following process.

Because large batches are produced, this intermediate buffer can cover sever-al days of production. This means that the material is not moved for more than 90% of the lead time, remaining parked in these intermediate buffers.

Depending on the product this can have an enormous cost effect on fixed capi-tal.

Each following production step is the cus-tomer of the preceding process section. Products are demanded by the customer based on their demand (in contrast to the Push System).

Introducing a Pull System reduces the inventory of work in process (WIP) and finished goods. This in turn reduces the lead time.

Again this causes a reduction of fixed capital and enhanced flexibility vis-à-vis the customer.

Push material flow

Pull material flow

The information flow begins when an order is accepted. The VSM docu-ments the type of communication (e.g. forecast, order, job) and the fre-quency (e.g. monthly, weekly). Communication types are visualized sym-bolically.

Symbols for the Information Flow

Electronic information:
type, frequency,
communication means

Manual information:
type, frequency,
communication means

DEFINE

MEASURE

ANALYZE

DESIGN

VERIFY

6. Add data boxes, determine the measurements and collect the data
All data for steering the process can be entered into the VSM data boxes.

The following process variables are usually recommended:
- Number of employees, number of shifts
- Processing time (P/T)
- Rework time
- Setup time (setup, SU or changeover C/O)
- Machine availability and / or OEE
- Yield
- Batch size
- Capacity
- Takt rate / takt time

Data Boxes

Material flow

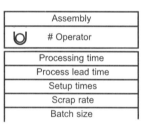

Process data

Customer data

After selecting the individual measurements, they are defined operationally. The data is then collected (if possible from the planning of the target process) and entered into the boxes.

7. Operationally define and identify the times
Adding the individual processing and waiting times in the process generates an estimated value for the total lead time of the value stream. The process lead time (PLT) describes the average time from the "raw material" to the "finished product". It is the key measurement for efficiency increase.

Processing and Idle Times

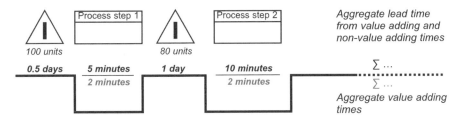

Value Stream Map

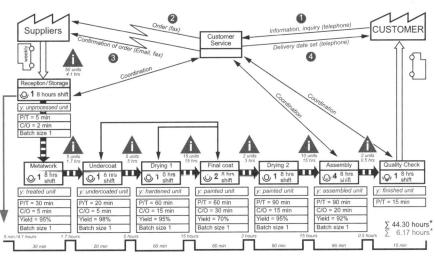

* *Non-value adding*
* *Value adding*

Standard operating procedures (SOPs) and production layout can be drawn up from the optimized and definitively defined process.

DEFINE

MEASURE

ANALYZE

DESIGN

VERIFY

Developing Standard Operating Procedures

📁 **Term/Description**

Standard Operating Procedures (SOPs), work instructions

🕐 **When**

In the Design Phase, developing a lean process

◎ **Goal**

Describe in detail the process steps from compiling the standard operating procedures to their introduction

▶▶ **Steps**

1. The following elements are needed to formulate standard operating procedures for the optimized or developed process:
   – Definition of process settings and material specifications
   – Coordination of Service Level Agreements (SLAs) with internal and external suppliers
   – Detailed description of process steps
   – Review the SOPs by a second person using defined and signed criteria
   – Information and training of employees
   – Sustainable change management
   – Definition of responsibilities

2. To ensure that the SOPs are easily understandable and suitable the following aspects need to be considered in the next step:
   – Apply a level of detail that explains which activities occur at what point in time and where
   – Graphic elements like process flow charts, flow charts and value stream maps etc. are to be used to pinpoint activities and results
   – Explain the reasons for the activity in simple language so that a stranger to the process can easily understand
   – Provide enough pointers (e.g. notes complimenting cause-effect relations) for restricting variation
   – Formulate explanations according to target group
   – Pay attention to simple and key access opportunities, i.e.:

DEFINE

- the SOP should be available not only online but also as a hard copy for everyone
- the responsibilities for the documentation of the activities must be defined clearly
- oportunities for internal link between the documentations must exist
- there should be a mechanism for updates and optimizations for the consistent further development of the documentation

MEASURE

Standard Operating Procedures

Example: passenger seat

Description of Activity:	Paint mixing	Process Step No.: 3	
INPUTS	List of Inputs:	Paint, color sample, order	
Paint mixing of amount required	Purpose: To ensure that the paint is available in the correct amount and quality while all relevant directives concerning safety at work and environment are met.		Duration: 60mins
			Equipment used: Mixing scale, color scale
	Customer: Paint shop		Special remarks:
	Responsible: Painter with order		None
	Place carried out: Paint room with mixing scale		
OUTPUT	List of Outputs:	Paint in the correct color	

Detailed Representation of Activities and Required Work Tools
Make all examples, forms, user interfaces etc. available

Activity:	Description:	Exception:	Remark:
Realization of what is required	To find out what is required check the order paper and enter the date into the order sheet.		
Adjustment of mixing scale			

ANALYZE

DESIGN

VERIFY

DEFINE

MEASURE

ANALYZE

DESIGN

VERIFY

Minimizing Process Lead Time

☐ Term/Description
Minimizing process lead time

⊙ When
In the Design Phase, developing and optimizing a lean process

◎ Goals
– Eliminate waste in the process
– Enhance the flexibility of the process

▶▶ Steps
1. Reduce complexity
2. Eliminate non-value adding activities
3. Reduce inventory and increase capacity at constraints
4. Reduce setup times

1. Reduce complexity
A key aspect of process design is to keep complexity at a minimum.
This should be considered in all areas of the process.

Avoiding Complexity

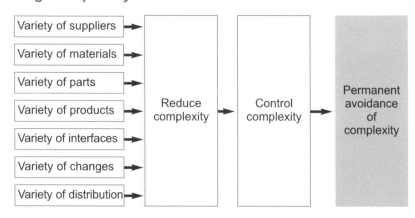

There are different possibilities for reducing complexity.

Possibilities for reducing complexity

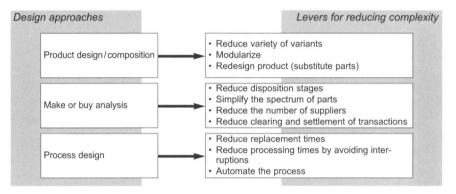

Design approaches	Levers for reducing complexity
Product design/composition	• Reduce variety of variants • Modularize • Redesign product (substitute parts)
Make or buy analysis	• Reduce disposition stages • Simplify the spectrum of parts • Reduce the number of suppliers • Reduce clearing and settlement of transactions
Process design	• Reduce replacement times • Reduce processing times by avoiding inter-ruptions • Automate the process

2. **Eliminate non-value adding activities**

   The process lead time is often largely determined by non-value adding activities.

Types of Waste in Production Processes

Seven types of waste in production	
1 **T**ransport	• Moving materials/products from one place to another • Repacking, transport on conveyor belts and bands etc. if the customer doesn't pay
2 **I**nventory	• Materials/products wait to be processed • Warehouse, buffer, temporary storage and illegal storage
3 **M**otion	• Superfluous movements/bad ergonomics • Workplaces far away from one another, search for materials, etc.
4 **W**aiting	• Delays within workflow • Waiting for material, releases, downtimes etc.
5 **O**verproduction	• More is produced than necessary • By avoiding setup procedures etc. • Using productivity as key control parameter
6 **O**verprocessing	• More is achieved than the customer is willing to pay for • By falsely understood and unknown customer needs etc.
7 **D**efects	• Defects which must be eliminated and/or scrap • Caused by false machine settings, materials, etc.

In the 1970s Taiichi Ohno, father of the Toyota production system, defined the seven types of waste (Acronym: TIMWOOD)

DEFINE

MEASURE

ANALYZE

DESIGN

VERIFY

Types of Waste in Service Processes

Seven types of waste in services	
1 **T**ransport	• Unnecessary transport of information • Moving documents, passing through hierarchies, unrequired filing
2 **I**nventory	• Unnecessary inventories • Documentation of concluded projects, unused working aids and data inventory, multiple filing
3 **M**otion	• Unnecessary ways • Distance covered when searching for documents, consulting colleagues, ergonomic obstacles
4 **W**aiting	• Waiting times / idle periods • Waiting for decisions, returns, passing on, warm-up time of office equipment
5 **O**verproduction	• Superfluous information • More information than the customer, the following processes or the current process phase require (emails, copies, memos, etc.)
6 **O**verprocessing	• Useless activities • Unread reports, statistics and protocols, unnecessary data entries and copies
7 **D**efects	• Errors • Media breaks in data formats, illegible faxes and notes, incomplete information

This approach is a key aspect when raising process efficiency.

$$\text{Process efficiency}\left[\%\right] = \frac{\text{Value adding time}\left[t\right]}{\text{Process lead time}\left[t\right]} \cdot 100\left[\%\right]$$

Process Lead Time

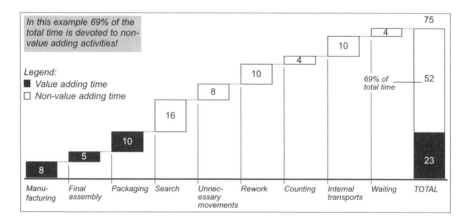

In this example 69% of the total time is devoted to non-value adding activities!

Legend:
■ Value adding time
□ Non-value adding time

300

DEFINE

3. Reducing inventory and raising capacity at constraints

Basic definitions:

Capacity
The maximum product amount (output) that a process produces within a specific period of time.

MEASURE

Bottlenecks (Time Trap)
The process step that causes the greatest delay in a process – there can only be one time trap in a process.

Constraint
A constraint is the process step that is incapable of producing the exit rate (internal or external) demanded by the customer (production below the takt rate oriented towards the customer need). A constraint is always a bottleneck, but a bottleneck doesn't always have to be a constraint!

Work in Process (WIP)
Inventory within the process; each complete operation that has begun but hasn't yet been finished. An operation can arise from materials, orders, waiting customers, assembling, emails, etc.

ANALYZE

Exit Rate
The output of a process within a specific time.

Takt Rate [quantity/time]
The quantity of a product (output) that the customer needs over a specific period of time.
Example: our customers demand a takt rate of 100 parts per day.

Takt Time [time/quantity]
The time span in which the process has to yield the produced units.
Example: the takt time is 45 seconds per part.

DESIGN

Existing constraints can be identified by using a Task Time Chart. The processing times of the respective process steps are collected in a diagram and related to the calculated takt time.

VERIFY

Task Time Chart

Example

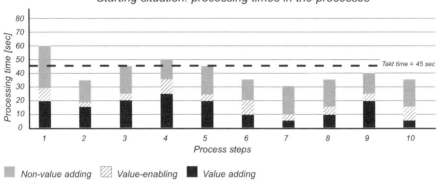

Starting situation: processing times in the processes

■ *Non-value adding* ▨ *Value-enabling* ■ *Value adding*

Constraints have an impact on the performance capability of a process because they require larger inventories, more machines, more personnel, more materials and more time to fulfill customer requirements.

Constraints can be avoided by reducing non-value adding activities, minimizing waste and merging single process steps.

The connection between process lead time, work in process (WIP) and process capability is described in Little's Law.

Little's Law

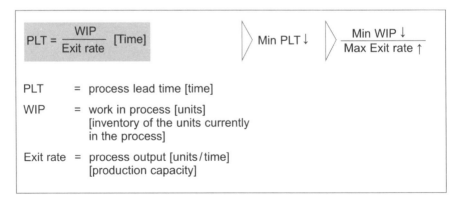

$$PLT = \frac{WIP}{Exit\ rate} \quad [Time]$$

$\rangle$ Min PLT ↓ $\rangle$ $\dfrac{\text{Min WIP} \downarrow}{\text{Max Exit rate} \uparrow}$

PLT   =   process lead time [time]

WIP   =   work in process [units]
                 [inventory of the units currently in the process]

Exit rate   =   process output [units / time]
                   [production capacity]

Reducing Process Lead Time

Example: production process with three process steps

Recording individual cycle times results in the following:

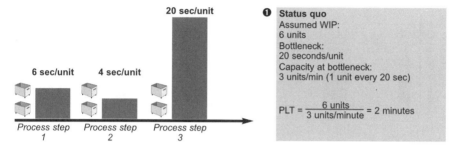

❶ Status quo
Assumed WIP:
6 units
Bottleneck:
20 seconds/unit
Capacity at bottleneck:
3 units/min (1 unit every 20 sec)

$$PLT = \frac{6 \text{ units}}{3 \text{ units/minute}} = 2 \text{ minutes}$$

How does reducing the WIP affect the process lead time in the production process while maintaining the same capacity?

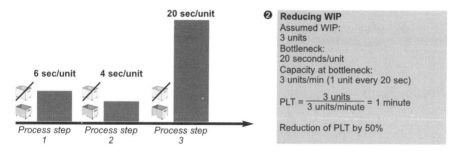

❷ Reducing WIP
Assumed WIP:
3 units
Bottleneck:
20 seconds/unit
Capacity at bottleneck:
3 units/min (1 unit every 20 sec)

$$PLT = \frac{3 \text{ units}}{3 \text{ units/minute}} = 1 \text{ minute}$$

Reduction of PLT by 50%

How does an additional capacity increase at the constraint affect the process lead time in the production process?

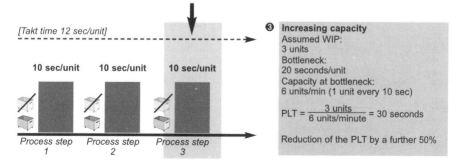

❸ Increasing capacity
Assumed WIP:
3 units
Bottleneck:
20 seconds/unit
Capacity at bottleneck:
6 units/min (1 unit every 10 sec)

$$PLT = \frac{3 \text{ units}}{6 \text{ units/minute}} = 30 \text{ seconds}$$

Reduction of the PLT by a further 50%

Process Balancing
Example

Real optimization approach

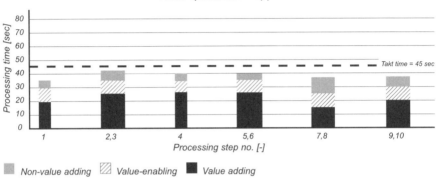

Non-value adding   Value-enabling   Value adding

4. Reduce setup times

The setup time is defined as the duration of time between the last good part of a batch until the first good part of the following batch, in accordance with planned process speed.

Setup Time
Example

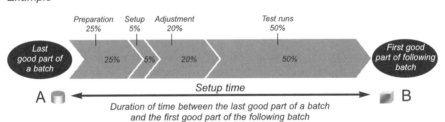

When the setup time is reduced internal setup actvities are focussed on.

Reducing setup time – also known as SMED (single minute exchange of die) – entails four steps:
1. Document the setup process and divide individual activities into internal and external activities

a. Internal setup activities can only be carried out when the machine is idle (e.g. exchange of tools)
b. External setup activities can be carried out parallel to an operating machine (e.g. preparing materials, invoicing batch)
2. Convert internal into external activities
3. Rationalize remaining internal activities
4. Eliminate adjustments and test runs

Four Steps for Setup Time Reduction in Batch Production

Short setup times are the key prerequisite for efficient production with small batch sizes

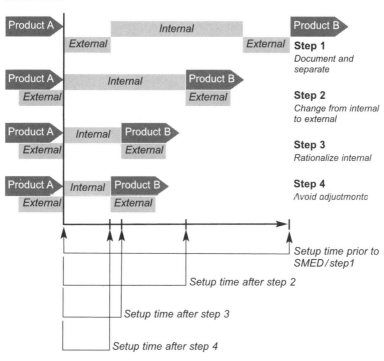

DEFINE

MEASURE

ANALYZE

DESIGN

VERIFY

Facility Layout Planning

📁 **Term / Description**

Plant Layout, Facility Layout Planning, Layout planning – for factory plants, facilities, buildings

🕓 **When**

In the Design Phase, developing a lean process

◎ **Goals**

Draw up a production layout by:
- Optimizing the internal distances to be covered
- Create an efficient working environment
- Guarantee process balance and control

▶▶ **Steps**

- Develop a layout for production process
- Draw up plans for manufacturing / offices
- Define and optimize the distance employees and materials have to cover
- Define the equipment of manufacturing / offices
- Integrate and ensure the 5 S concept
- Review and budget environmental, health and safety standards (e.g. ventilation, separate ways etc.)
- Analyze material and information flow within the individual process variables to identify optimization opportunities in the specific working environment

Spaghetti Diagram

🗀 Term/Description
Spaghetti Diagram

🕗 When
In the Design Phase, developing a lean process

◎ Goals
- Clarify planned material and information flows
- Detect optimization potentials

▶▶ Steps
The paths necessary for conventional production are marked on a layout plan with the help of production process.
The different colors represent employees, materials and/or information.

Spaghetti Diagram

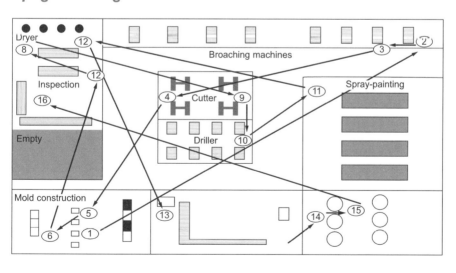

5 S Concept

☐ **Term / Description**

5 S: sort – seiri; set in order – seiton; shine – seiso; standardize – seiketsu; sustain – shitsuke

🕐 **When**

In the Design Phase, developing lean process

◎ **Goals**

Create a clean, safe and efficient working environment

▶▶ **Steps**

Five Japanese words stand for the principles of a well-organized working environment:

– **Seiri – sort, separate**
All objects at the workplace are sorted into the categories "necessary" and "unnecessary". (Unnecessary objects are eliminated.)

– **Seiton – set in order, simplify**
All objects at the workplace are assigned a permanent place where they are found quickly and easily.

– **Seiso – shine, scrub**
The working environment is kept clean and tidy.

– **Seiketsu – standardize**
A standard defines sustainable order and cleanliness.

– **Shitsuke – systematize, sustain, self-discipline**
The described procedures become a habit.

Implementing 5 S can be visualized in a Radar Chart:

5S Radar Chart

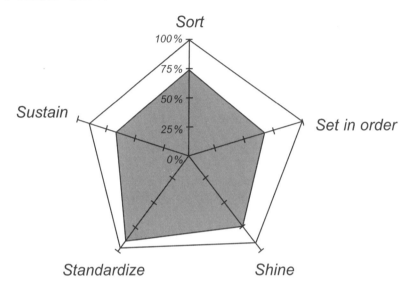

Planning the Equipment

🗀 **Term / Description**
Operational Equipment Planning

🕓 **When**
In the Design Phase, developing lean process

◎ **Goals**
- Identify the necessary machines, equipment and tools
- Optimize availability of machines and equipments

▸▸ **Steps**
- Define the requirements to the machines, equipments and tools
- Select the machines, equipments and tools
- If necessary develop the tools
- Test the machines at the manufacturer
- Plan and optimize setup procedures
- Test maintenance
- Draw up a maintenance plan
- Determine the need of replacement parts

Planning Material Procurement

📁 **Term / Description**
Material Procurement Planning

🕒 **When**
In the Design Phase, developing lean process

◎ **Goal**
– Ensure that materials are procured at the right time, in the right amount, in the quality required and at minimal costs

▶▶ **Steps**
– Draw up procedures for testing quality
– Determine the amounts for consumption and purchasing expenditures
– Select suppliers
– Determine the service level agreements with suppliers

⇒ **Tip**
The earlier possible errors are detected the lower are their elimination costs. There are different **"examination methods"** *(see Poka Yoke)* which help to detect errors in a process at an early stage.

DEFINE

MEASURE

ANALYZE

DESIGN

VERIFY

Making Employees Available

☐ Term / Description

Personnel Planning, Work Plan, Work Organization

🕓 When

In the Design Phase, developing lean process

◎ Goal

Plan personnel by meeting the demands to implement the new processes

▶▶ Steps

- Define workplaces and activities
- Define work organization
- Derive the necessary skills and abilities
- Determine how much personnel is required
- Set a training plan
- Test workplace layout, test stress of employees (environment, health and safety) and ergonomics
- Define wages and incentive systems

⇨ Tips

A suitable training concept should answer the following questions:

- Which working steps are primarily influenced by the changeover?
- Who is responsible for these working steps and who carries them out?
- Who is the internal supplier or customer of the process step?
- How can these persons be prepared for the changeover?
- How can an optimal transfer of training contents to everyday work be guaranteed?
- How can the changeover be communicated outwards (elevator speech)?

Implementation teams are formed in the trainings. These teams support the changeover in a variety of ways, acting as multipliers:

- They ensure the communication of the changeover activities in their respective departments.

DEFINE

- They secure the complete changeover to the new process by acting as contact partners on site.
- They report implementation risks and problems to the DFSS team at an early stage.

MEASURE

ANALYZE

DESIGN

VERIFY

DEFINE

Providing IT

☐ **Term / Description**
Supply and demand for information technology, IT provision

🕓 **When**
In the Design Phase, developing lean process

◎ **Goal**
Ensure functioning design of IT meeting the demands to depict the new processes

▶▶ **Steps**
- Collect the requirements to IT
- Ensure its compliance with existing systems
- Develop logical and physical design
- Define hardware and software
- Test data migration
- Train employees

To ensure a need-based design of IT performance, the performance scope for describing the processes must be determined in advance. There are three areas which IT can take over:

- Technical infrastructure:
  The hardware and its performance features, i.e. all the tasks involving the operation of the central processor and the computer systems.
- Software and system structure:
  This area covers applications, their development and adjustment, as well as maintenance work.
- IT personnel
  Qualitative and quantitative personnel capacity because the IT area in particular is characterized by expertise and communication.

MEASURE

ANALYZE

DESIGN

VERIFY

Optimizing Lean Process Design

📁 **Term / Description**
Process Design Optimization

🕐 **When**
In the Design Phase, optimizing lean process

◎ **Goal**
Evaluate and optimize the developed process in terms of quality, capacity and costs

⏩ **Steps**
1. Review the layouts defined for the lean process in terms of their quality, capacity and costs

Evaluation Matrix

Design element	Evaluation					Evaluation:
	1	2	3	4	5	1 = is fulfilled by 0%
Processes				⬤	⬤	2 = is fulfilled by 25%
Facilities / buildings				⬤	⬤	3 = is fulfilled by 50%
Equipment				⬤	⬤	4 = is fulfilled by 75%
Materials				⬤	⬤	5 = is fulfilled by 100%
Employees				⬤	⬤	
IT				⬤	⬤	
Are regulatory requirements met?				✓		

Criteria:
◯ Quality
⬤ Costs
⬤ Capacity

2. Optimize the lean process using specific lean tools and improve the quality by applying statistical methods, e.g. DOE.
3. Identify, analyze and wherever possible eliminate risks, for example by using an FMEA.

DEFINE

MEASURE

ANALYZE

DESIGN

VERIFY

Gate Review

📁 **Term / Description**

Gate Review, phase check, phase assessment

🕐 **When**

At the conclusion of each phase

◎ **Goals**

- Inform the Sponsor about the results and measures taken in the respective phase
- Assess the results
- Decide on the further steps and activities of the project

▶▶ **Steps**

The results are presented completely and in an easily comprehensible form. The Sponsor is to examine the status of the project on the basis of the following criteria:

- Results are complete,
- Probability of project success,
- Resources are optimally allocated in the project.

The Sponsor decides if the project can enter the next phase.

All results from the Design Phase are presented to the Sponsor and Stakeholders in the Gate Review. The following questions must be answered in a complete and comprehensible presentation:

DEFINE

MEASURE

ANALYZE

On developing, testing and optimizing the detailed design concept:
- Were Transfer Functions for evaluating the design parameters developed? What are they?
- Were alternative characteristics defined for the design elements determined and compared to one another?
  Which statistically significant differences were detected?
- Were Tolerance Design and Design for X applied?
  What was the result?
- Has a design scorecard been developed for the detailed concept?
- Was a prototype implemented?
  What insights could be derived from this?
- Were the test results worked into the final design and if so, how?
- Which risks were identified and which measures for risk prevention were derived?
- Was the market launch prepared? In which way?

On testing the performance capacity of the process and input variables:
- Were the relevant process and input variables identified?
- Have the relevant process and input variables been tested?
  What was the result?
- Has the current performance capacity of the process been evaluated?
  How were they evaluated?

On developing the Lean Process:
- Has the process design been drawn up?
- Were all regulatory requirements considered?
- Was all process-related data entered into a VSM?
- Was the process efficiency reviewed and optimized?
  Which tools were used?
- Was a production layout developed?
  How was it tested and what was the result?
- How was the material procurement planned?
  Which measures were introduced to ensure the consistent quality of suppliers?
- How is the availability of the employees ensured?
  How is their ability and motivation guaranteed?
- Which IT resources support the lean process?

DESIGN

VERIFY

DEFINE

MEASURE

ANALYZE

DESIGN

VERIFY

Calculating costs and formulating marketing strategies:
- How have the detailed product costs been itemized?
- Which production costs (PC1) have been calculated?
- Which quality costs are expected (rework, scrap, etc.)?
- Have the target costs been met?
- What are the key features of the detailed marketing and sales plan? Which costs have been calculated for it?
- Which contribution margin (CM1 to CM4) were calculated?

Design for Six Sigma^{+Lean} Toolset

Toolset

VERIFY

DEFINE

MEASURE

ANALYZE

DESIGN

VERIFY

Phase 5: Verify

Goals

- Pilot and implement the new process
- Develop a suitable process management
- Hand over responsibility for the process

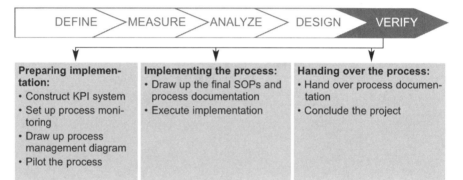

| DEFINE | MEASURE | ANALYZE | DESIGN | VERIFY |

Preparing implemen-tation:
- Construct KPI system
- Set up process moni-toring
- Draw up process management diagram
- Pilot the process

Implementing the process:
- Draw up the final SOPs and process documentation
- Execute implementation

Handing over the process:
- Hand over process documen-tation
- Conclude the project

Steps

The implementation and the handover to the Process Owner occurs after the successful piloting.

A roadmap for the Verify Phase is presented on the opposite page.

Most Important Tools

- PDCA Cycle
- FMEA
- Project Management Tools (Work Packages, Gantt Chart, Network Plan, RACI Chart)
- Change Management Tools (Stakeholder Analysis, Communication Plan)
- Documentation
- SOPs
- KPI Systems
- Control Charts
- Process Management Diagram

Verify Roadmap

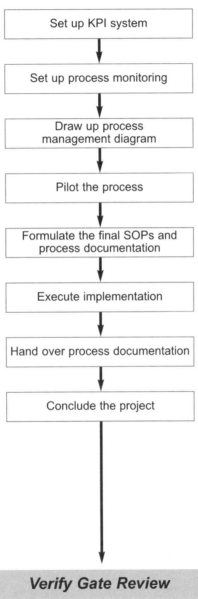

DEFINE

MEASURE

ANALYZE

DESIGN

VERIFY

DEFINE

MEASURE

ANALYZE

DESIGN

VERIFY

Preparing Implementation

📁 **Term / Description**
Implementation Planning, Implementation Strategy

🕐 **When**
In the Verify Phase, planning implementation

◎ **Goals**
– Derive the implementation strategy
– Finalize implementation plan

▶▶ **Steps**
The implementation plan is added and finalized. An implementation plan covers a wide variety of contents.

Contents of an Implementation Plan

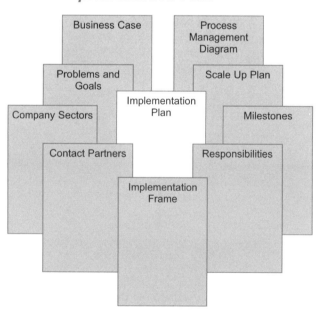

The **Implementation Frame** defines the borders of the implementation project.

Implementation Frame

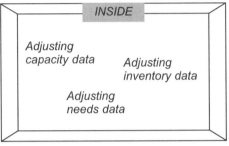

Implementation frame

A **Scale Up Plan** avoids errors in complex changeovers these are introduced step-by-step and, optimized if necessary.

Scale Up Steps

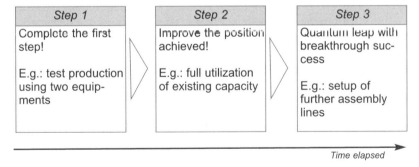

Multigeneration Plans also support a structured implementation planning. A Transition Plan helps to avoid idle and downtimes during changeover. This can be achieved in different ways.

A Transition Plan is presented on the following page.

DEFINE

MEASURE

ANALYZE

DESIGN

VERIFY

Transition Plan

Dislocation	Parallel Operation	Step-by-Step Transition
Shutdown and dislocation of the current operating process to an alternative location until the changeover to the new process is completed	Parallel operation of the old and new process until the process is stable and reliable.	Exploitation of production time with low level of machine utilization to carry out the changeover to the new process step-by-step.

The controllability of the new process must be guaranteed. The control of process-relevant data is secured by a Process Management Diagram.

Process Management Diagram

Process Management	Monitoring	Reaction Plan
• Secure the controllability of the process • Define the process steps, KPIs, target values, specifications, and necessary actions	• Present the selected KPIs in Run Charts and Control Charts • Prepare regular reporting (IT support)	• Define the necessary measures if deviations occur • Prepare training measures for the employees

A variety of strategies is possible for implementing the process.

Implementation Strategies

In Phases	The process design is implemented and realized step-by-step at one location in line with defined implementation phases
Sequential	The defined process design is implemented and realized initially at one location before it is implemented at another location
Holistic	An integrated implementation of the defined process design is undertaken simultaneously at all locations

It makes sense to combine these implementation strategies with one another. The following questions are helpful:
– How much time is available for implementing the process?
– Which projects or initiatives are affected by implementation? To what extent?
– Which projects or initiatives can be integrated as support?
– Which resources are required for the respective implementation strategy?
– What consequences result from the implementation on current operations?

The implementation of the lean process should be prepared thoroughly:
– All of the areas affected by the new process design must be identified.
– An implementation frame has to be set.
– Contact partners and persons responsible for implementation must be named.
– The need for transition plans must be evaluated.

DEFINE

MEASURE

ANALYZE

DESIGN

VERIFY

Setting up KPI System

📁 **Term / Description**
KPI System, Key Performance Indicators

🕐 **When**
In the Verify Phase, planning implementation

◎ **Goals**
– Identify the degree of added value for the newly developed products and processes
– Monitor and manage the whole value adding process

▶▶ **Steps**
1. The supply chain is divided into the areas procurement, production and distribution

2. Performance indicators are determined for each area; these provide an evaluation and if required a control of the specific performance and performance potentials.

Controlling the Value Added Chain

> Value adding process

KPIs for the supply chain area

Order disposition and materials logistics	Planning and controlling target production	Sales planning and controlling, processing customer orders
KPI for procurement	KPI for production	KPI for distribution

DEFINE

Relevant KPIs for procurement
The KPIs controlling the whole procurement process have to include key figures from all stages of the value added chain.

Relevant KPIs for Procurement

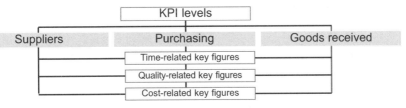

It is recommended to define the following KPIs:
- Influencing factors which affect the performance of procurement
- Demand, the quantity and the point in time of procurement (short- and long-term)
- Procurement costs of materials
- Purchasing payments and securing material supply

MEASURE

Procurement Matrix
Example: passenger seat

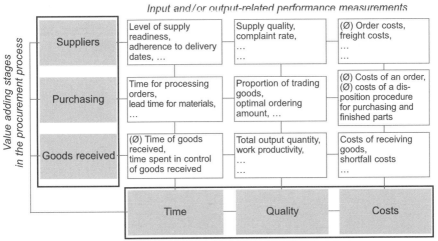

ANALYZE

DESIGN

VERIFY

Relevant KPIs for production

A KPI system in the production area should provide information about the following aspects:

– The development tendencies of the process
– Efficiency, reliability and accuracy of production activities
– Relations between the single activities
– Optimization potentials in the production area

Production Matrix

Example: passenger seat

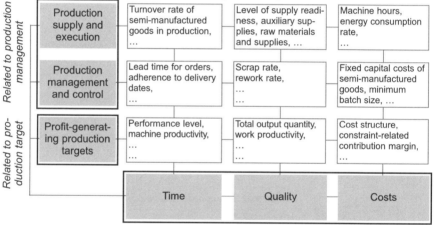

Control and optimization criteria

Relevant KPIs for distribution
Suitable key figures for the KPI system in distribution enable:
- Transparency in relation to quality and costs
- Identification of optimization potential
- Securing the sustainability of improvements

Distribution Matrix
Example: passenger seat

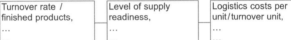

Input and/or output-related performance measurements

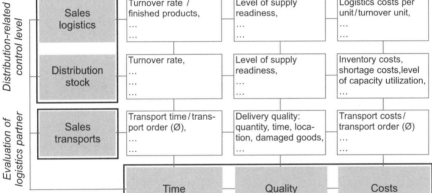

Control and optimization criteria

Setting up Process Monitoring

☐ **Term/Description**
Monitoring, process monitoring

🕐 **When**
In the Verify Phase, planning implementation

◎ **Goals**
Monitor process capability

▶▶ **Steps**
After the KPIs were selected the regular recording and monitoring of the individual key figures is to be introduced.
The following procedure is chosen:

1. Ensure standardized capturing of the key figures (What? How? When? How often? Where? Who?)

2. Set the specification limits (specified by customers):

   LSL = lower specification limit;
   USL = upper specification limit.

3. Use Control Charts to determine the control limits statistically:

   LCL = lower control limit ($\approx$ - 3 standard deviations from mean value);
   UCL = upper control limit ($\approx$ + 3 standard deviations from mean value).

   Overall 99.74% of the data lies in the interval between the upper and lower control limits. If a data point lies outside this interval or reveals a strong tendency (see Shewart's rules), a statistical outlier exists – it may be assumed that a special cause exists. This must be examined in detail.

DEFINE

4. Monitor process capability. There are four possibilities:
   A. The process is within the specifications and under control statistically: no action is required.
   B. The process is not within the specifications but is under control statistically: search for common causes and optimize the process.
   C. The process is within the specifications but not under control statistically: monitor the process closely.
   D. The process is not within the specifications and is not under control statistically: search for special causes and carry out "fire prevention" measures.

MEASURE

Monitoring
Example: passenger seat

Key figure	No. of defective seat covers	
Definition	No. of defective seat covers in relation to the total number of produced seats	
Dimension	%	
Target value	Target value 1% per year	
Measurement poriod	Weekly	
Repeat	Permanent measurent	
Data collector	Quality control	
Data receiver	Process owner	
Evaluation / reporting	Head of quality control	
Responsible	Process owner	

—♦— *Percent in the measurement week*
—■— *Target for the measurement week*

ANALYZE

DESIGN

VERIFY

DEFINE

MEASURE

ANALYZE

DESIGN

VERIFY

Monitoring Process Capability

 A

In the specification limits and under statistical control

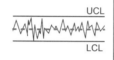

No action necessary

B

Not within the specification limits but under statistical control

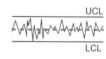

Action: optimize the process

C

In the specification limits but not under statistical control

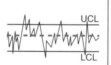

Monitor closely, for the time being no action necessary

D

Not in the specification limits and not under statistical control

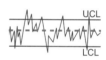

Action: fire prevention – find the causes for the outliers and eliminate them

LSL = lower specification limit: the lower limits specified by the customer

USL = upper specification limit: the upper limits specified by the customer

LCL = lower control limit: the lower control limits calculated statistically

UCL = upper control limit: the upper control limits calculated statistically

⇨ **Tip**
- Monitoring supported visually by images, colors and markings ensures sustainability.
- The process owners are to be trained in handling the process monitoring.

Drawing up Process Management Diagram

📁 **Term / Description**
Process Management Diagram

🕲 **When**
In the Verify Phase, preparing implementation

◎ **Goals**
- If the figures exceed or fall below the specifications the action to be taken is clear
- A targeted reaction and the initiation of appropriate measures are possible
- Consistent process control

▶▶ **Steps**
1. Examine improved processes, e.g. with the aid of an FMEA, for potential problems.
2. Deduce the necessary measures for each point and nominate the responsible person.
3. Compile a process management diagram (process mapping, monitoring with KPI and reaction plan).
4. Monitor the process – the reaction plan is launched as soon as deviations are evident.
5. Once the KPIs were determined the individual key figures are to be captured and monitored regularly.

An example of a Process Management Diagram is presented on the following page.

DEFINE

MEASURE

ANALYZE

DESIGN

VERIFY

DEFINE MEASURE ANALYZE DESIGN VERIFY

Process Management Diagram

Process: Paintshop / accident repair					Process Owner: F. Flintstone				Date: April 2007	
Purpose: Maintenance of paint quality in accident repairs									Revision: 17.5	

Process Steps					Monitoring				Reaction Plan	
Dept. A	Dept. B	Dept. C	Dept. D	Dept. E	Output Measurements	Input and Process Measurements	Standard Specification	Method of Sampling Recording Data	Immediate Solution	Process/System Improvement
Order to repair					Understandability of the order		100% of the employees with full understanding	Weekly questioning of employees by measuring group		Monthly checking by customer service manager
	Repair of bodywork				Duration of repair		Bodywork start at least 4 days before completion date	Weekly sample comparison of completion date and repair completion date by measuring group		Monthly checking by customer service manager
						Availability of spare parts	95% availability at the start of work	Full collection of data through IT, through person responsible for bodywork in warehouse	One person in warehouse is nominated as person responsible	
		Spraypainting			Paint thickness in micrometers		Paint thickness not more than 300 micrometers	Full collection of data through measurement by dept. head at the final control		Monthly checking by customer service manager
					Durability of paint		No rusting through paint within 5 years	Writing to the affected customers after 2, 4 and 5 years	Monthly form letter action steered by IT and date	Discussion of results in a monthly management meeting
					Number of internal rework		Maximum 2% in 90 days	Following monthly finance reports from the dept. head paintwork		Part of quality management reviews
					Department gross turnover			Following monthly finance reports from the dept. head paintwork		
						Availability of required paint		Full collection of data through IT, through person responsible for bodywork in warehouse	One person in warehouse is nominated as person responsible	

Piloting the Process

📁 **Term / Description**
Pilot, testing the new process in a limited environment

🕓 **When**
In the Verify Phase, preparing implementation

◎ **Goals**
- Test the performance capability of the developed process
- Create the basis for the Roll Out

⏩ **Steps**
Piloting a process comprises four steps, Plan – Do – Check – Act (PDCA):

1	Plan: prepare the pilot
2	Do: carry out the pilot
3	Check: analyze the results
4	Act: carry out optimization

1. Plan: prepare the pilot
Activities necessary for preparing the pilot:
- Name the pilot team
- Define the pilot scope
- Draw up an implementation plan
- Estimate the risks
- Provide facilities and buildings
- Procure and set up machines and equipment
- Set up IT infrastructure
- Procure sufficient amounts of material from the selected suppliers
- Train employees on the job

Use a process FMEA (see Analyze) to identify and analyze potential errors in advance. Strategies are then developed for the early detection and avoidance of such defect opportunities.

In this way an FMEA can serve as the basis for a reaction plan.

2. Do: carry out the pilot
To enable an early correction the pilot is to be carried out step-by-step:
- Prepare test runs
- Carry out test runs
- Optimize machine settings (DOE)
- Raise the amounts step-by-step
- Raise production to full load

3. Check: analyze results
For the process analysis each relevant step is viewed under the following aspects:
- Quality (compliance with specifications, process capability)
- Capacity (exit rate, speed)
- Costs (target costs achieved?)
- Regulatory requirements (environment, health, safety at work)

Various parameters can be used to evaluate the process.

Parameters for Validating a Process

Validating process steps		
Quality	Specifications	LSL, USL
	Process capability	C_p, C_{pk}, LCL, UCL
Capacity	Exit rate	Quantity / time
	Speed	Process lead time
Costs	Production costs	Materials, personnel costs, etc
	Working capital	Inventory in euros (working capital and finished goods inventories)
	Fixed assets	Depreciation of machines, buildings, etc.
Regulatory requirements	Environment	Emissions
	Health	Ergonomics and stress
	Safety at work	Danger of injury

DEFINE

4. **Act: carry out optimizations**

   If the results do not match the planned targets, the weak points are to be eliminated. After eliminating these, the PDCA cycle begins again – until the desired results are achieved. Afterwards the release for the Roll Out can occur.

Pilot Program and PDAC
Example: passenger seat

MEASURE

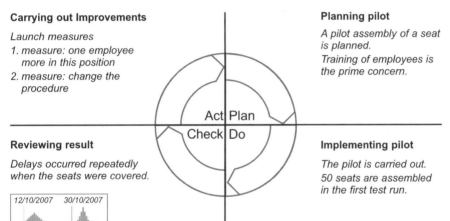

Carrying out Improvements

Launch measures
1. *measure: one employee more in this position*
2. *measure: change the procedure*

Planning pilot

A pilot assembly of a seat is planned.
Training of employees is the prime concern.

Reviewing result

Delays occurred repeatedly when the seats were covered.

12/10/2007	30/10/2007
▂▃▄▃▁	▁▄▃▂▁
PLT in hours	

Implementing pilot

The pilot is carried out.
50 seats are assembled in the first test run.

ANALYZE

DESIGN

VERIFY

DEFINE

Drawing up Final SOPs and Process Documentation

MEASURE

📁 **Term / Description**
Standard Operating Procedures (SOPs), Process Documentation

🕐 **When**
In the Verify Phase, implementing the process

◎ **Goal**
Secure the sustainability of the project result

ANALYZE

▶▶ **Steps**
1. After the pilot was successfully carried out all changes are incorporated into the process documentation and the SOPs.

2. These are then made accessible at the respective workplaces:
   – Use methods of the visual process control, visual presentation of the optimal workplace based on 5S, visual plotting of the most important movements and correctly finished products.
   – Visualize the most important production parameters like machine settings, takt, WIP, process lead times, etc.

DESIGN

VERIFY

Carrying out Implementation

📁 **Term / Description**
Implementation, Roll Out

🕐 **When**
In the Verify Phase, implementing the process

◎ **Goal**
Create non-defective products with an efficient and effective process

▶▶ **Steps**
In order to optimally roll out the solution elaborated and verified in the course of the project, planning and executing implementation focuses on the key requirements of a project:

1. **Goals of implementation** are defined on the basis of a Project Charter:
   – Why is the implementation carried out?
   – What is to be achieved with implementation?
   – Which restrictions have proven to be necessary?

2. **Activities, time and resource planning** are identified with the aid of the presented tools:
   – Definition of activities (*see Define Phase*)
   – Determination of times
   – Determination of responsibilities
   – Visualization in a Gantt Chart

3. **Budget planning and control** from two viewpoints:
   – Is the budget planned for implementation kept (procurement costs, training costs, installation, etc.)?
   – Are the planned production costs kept (energy, work, maintenance, etc.)?

4. **Risk estimation** can occur with the following tools:
   – Process FMEA (see Analyze)
   – Risk Management Matrix (see Define)

DEFINE

MEASURE

ANALYZE

DESIGN

VERIFY

5. **Change Management strategy** is developed on the basis of the following procedure:
   - Stakeholder Analysis (*see Define*)
   - Communication Plan (*see Define*)

6. **Management and Control** enable an efficient and plannable implementation through:
   - RACI Charts (*see Define*)
   - Monitoring
   - Reaction Plan when deviations occur

Handing over Process Documentation

📁 **Term / Description**
Handover, Process Handover, process is handed over to process owner

🕑 **When**
In the Verify Phase, handing over the process

◎ **Goals**
– Handover of process to the owner
– Official closure of the project

▶▶ **Steps**
The process owners take over responsibility for the developed process once the project has been handed over. An efficient process management is based on the long-term gathering and analysis of all relevant data:

– Final documentation and SOPs
– Relevant KPIs and control parameters
– Regular and correct monitoring
– Process management (incl. necessary Reaction Plan)
– Introduce the process owners to the Process Management Diagram

DEFINE

MEASURE

ANALYZE

DESIGN

VERIFY

Carrying out Project Closure

📁 **Term / Description**
Project Closure

🕐 **When**
In the Verify Phase, handing over the process

◎ **Goals**
– Officially hand over the project documentation
– Closure of the project

▶▶ **Steps**
– All project documentations are summarized. The contents and structure should be drawn up in such a way that:
  - the experience and the knowledge of the team are maintained and can be used further for examples of Best Practice.
  - A basis for other development projects in the company is developed.
  - The results and data are recorded for later comparisons.

  Both the results of the project as well as the work of the development team are to be evaluated and communicated with respect to the following questions:
  - What was learned in the course of project work?
  - What can be done better in subsequent projects?

Lessons Learned Matrix

Team/Resources	Schedule
• Were the team and the resources available? • Was the planning adhered to? • What contributed positively to the plan being adhered to and should be repeated in the next project? • What had a negative effect and should be avoided in the next project?	• Was the schedule kept? • What contributed positively to the schedule being kept and should be repeated in the next project? • What had a negative effect and should be avoided in the next project?
Goals/Results	Further Important Points
• Was the goal achieved? • What contributed positively to the goal being adhered to and should be repeated in the next project? • What had a negative effect and should be avoided in the next project?	• What other factors were advantageous and should be repeated in the next project? • What was a hindrance and should be avoided in future?

DEFINE

MEASURE

ANALYZE

DESIGN

VERIFY

Gate Review

🗀 **Term / Description**
Gate Review, phase closure

🕑 **When**
At the conclusion of each phase

◎ **Goals**
– Inform the Sponsor about the results and measures taken in the respective phase
– Assess the results
– Decide on the further course of the project

▶▶ **Steps**
The results are presented completely and in an easily comprehensible form. The Sponsor is to examine the current status of the project on the basis of the following criteria:
– Results are complete,
– Probability of project success,
– Resources are optimally allocated in the project.

All results from the Verify Phase are presented to the Sponsor and Stakeholders in the Verify Gate Review. To enable the closure of the Verify Phase and the handover of the project by the Sponsor, the following questions need to be answered:

344

DEFINE

MEASURE

ANALYZE

DESIGN

VERIFY

On piloting:
- How successfully was the pilot carried out?
- How well have the goals concerning quality, costs and capacity been achieved and are the regulatory requirements fulfilled?

On implementing:
- How was the process documented at last?
- Is the process monitored by a sensible KPI system?
- How are tests carried out to verfy if the Reaction Plan is functioning in case deviations occur?
- Have the activities necessary for the market launch been carried out successfully?
- How can one ascertain if these activities are sufficient?

On process handover:
- What are the contents of the final documentation?
- What signalizes that the process owner has assumed full responsibility and the development team is now released from its tasks?

Costs calculation and marketing:
- How are the detailed product costs itemized?
- Which production costs (PC1) were calculated?
- Which quality costs are expected (rework, scrap, etc.)?
- Are the target costs fulfilled?
- What are the features of the detailed marketing and sales plan? Which costs were calculated for them?
- Which contribution margin (CM1 to CM2) have been calculated?

The project can be closed officially now!

Time to celebrate!

5S	Sort / Set in Order / Shine / Standardize / Sustain
AFD	Anticipatory Failure Detection
AHP	Analytic Hierarchy Process
ANOVA	Analysis of Variances
BB	Black Belt
C/O	Changeover (Setup Time)
CAD	Computer-aided Design
CAPS	Computer-aided Process Simulation
CIT	Change Implementation Tools
CTB	Critical to Business
CTQ	Critical to Quality
DFC	Design for Configuration
DFE	Design for Environment
DFMA	Design for Manufacturing and Assembly
DFR	Design for Reliability
DFS	Design for Services
DFSS	Design for Six Sigma
DMADV	Define, Measure, Analyze, Design, Verify
DMAIC	Define, Measure, Analyze, Improve, Control
DOE	Design of Experiments
DPMO	Defects per Million Opportunities
DPU	Defects per Unit
EBIT	Earnings before Interest and Taxes
EBITDA	Earnings before Interest, Taxes, Depreciation and Amortization
EHS	Environment / Health / Safety
etc.	et cetera
EVA®	Economic Value Added
FMEA	Failure Mode and Effect Analysis
FTA	Fault Tree Analysis
GB	Green Belt
HR	Human Resources
IT	Information Technology
KPI	Key Performance Indicator

LCL	Lower Control Limit
LSL	Lower Specification Limit
Max	Maximum
MBB	Master Black Belt
MCA	Monte Carlo Analysis
MGP	Multigeneration Plan
min	Minimum
NOPAT	Net Operating Profit after Taxes
PLT	Process Lead Time
P/T	Processing Time
PDCA	Plan, Do, Check, Act
ppm	Parts per million
QFD	Quality Function Diagram
R&D	Research & Development
R&R	Repeatability & Reproducibility
RACI	Responsible / Accountable / Consulted / Informed
RPN / RPZ	Risk Priority Number
RSS	Root Sum Square Method
RTY	Rolled Throughput Yield
SCAMPER	Substitute / Combine / Adapt / Modify / Put to other uses / Eliminate
SIPOC	Supplier / Input / Prozess / Output / Customer
SLA	Service Level Agreements
SMA	Shape-Memory Alloys
SMED	Single Minute Exchange of Die
SU	Setup
Sufield Analysis	Substance-Field Analysis
TIMWOOD	Transport / Inventory / Motion / Waiting / Overproduction / Overprocessing / Defects
TIPS	Theory of Inventive Problem Solving
TRIZ	Teoriya Reshemiya Izobretatelskikh Zadach (Russian acronym for TIPS)

UCL	Upper Control Limit
USL	Upper Specification Limit
USP	Unique Selling Proposition / Point
VOC	Voice of Customer
VSM	Value Stream Map
WCA	Worst Case Analysis
WIP	Work in Process

Term	Page
C	
CAD Method	253
Cash Flow	18, 31
Change Management	22, 40 et seq., **52**, 55, 296, 320, 340
Changeover (C/O)	294, 312 et seq., 323 et seq., 347
Computer-aided Design	244, 253, 347
Communication Plan	14, 22, 51 et seq., 320, 340
Communication Process	51 et seq.
Competition Analysis	26, 52, 64
Competition Comparison	101
Complexity Reduction	**204**, 243, 298 et seq.
Concept, Selecting the Best	14, 47, 134 et seq., **155 et seq.**
Concept, Finalizing the	134 et seq., **227**
Concept FMEA	218, 223, 234
Concept Review	229
Confidence Interval	256 et seqq, 263
Confidence Level	256, 272
Conjoint Analysis	155, **160 et seqq.**, 163 et seqq.
Constraint	301, 303, 328
Contradiction Matrix	176, **184 et seq.**, Appendix
Control Charts	250, 286, 290, 320, 324, 330
Correlation Matrix	104, **114 et seqq.**, 168
Cost Monitoring	48
Cost Planning	48
C_{pk}-value	**124 et seqq.**
C_p-value	**124 et seqq.**
Creativity Techniques	14, 134, 145, 236, 238, 244
CTQs	14, 42 et seqq., 60, 98, 103 et seq., 109, 111 et seq., 117, 131, 136, 141 et seq., 156, 168, 186, 240, 243, 248, 272, 283
Customer Feedback	14 et seq., 217, 219, 226, 234
Customer Interaction Study	14, 60 et seq., 70, **73 et seqq.**, 79, 81, 131
Customer Needs, Identifying	**85**

Term	Page
R	
RACI Chart	14, 22, 33, 45, **46**
Ranking	109, 162, 165 et seq., 206, 271
Rapid Method	253
Rapid Growth	208
Reaction Plan	42, 324, 333 et seq., 336, **340 et seq.**, 345
Research Methods	60 et seq., **69**, 71
Redesign	23 et seq., **28**, 30, 287, 299
Relative Functionality	206
Relationship Matrix	104f, 109, 110 et seq., 168
Response Optimizer	167, 269, 273
Respondents, Selecting Sample/Survey	80 et seq., 161
Risk Assessment	40, **54**
Risk Evaluation	**117 et seq., 218, 276**
Risk Evaluation Matrix	**118**
Risk Classification	55
Risk Management Matrix	**54**, 227, **228**, 339
Risk Priority Number (RPN)	219 et seq., 348
Roadmap Analyze	135
Roadmap Define	23
Roadmap Design	237
Roadmap Measure	61
ROI	31
Roll Out	15, 47, 335, 337, 339
Rolled Throughput Yield (RTY)	122 et seq.
Roles	16, 22 et seq., 24 et seq., 41, 46, 56, 58
Root Sum Square Method (RSS)	348
RPN (Risk Priority Number)	219 et seq., 348
S	
Sample	70, 81, 126, 250, 255 et seqq., 261 et seqq., 324, 334
Sample Size	81, 128, 250, 256 et seq.
Satisfier	93, 105

Yield	Process Sigma (ST)	Defects per 1,000,000	Defects per 100,000	Defects per 10,000	Defects per 1,000	Defects per 100
99,99966%	6,0	3,4	0,34	0,034	0,0034	0,00034
99,9995%	5,9	5	0,5	0,05	0,005	0,0005
99,9992%	5,8	8	0,8	0,08	0,008	0,0008
99,9990%	5,7	10	1	0,1	0,01	0,001
99,9980%	5,6	20	2	0,2	0,02	0,002
99,9970%	5,5	30	3	0,3	0,03	0,003
99,9960%	5,4	40	4	0,4	0,04	0,004
99,9930%	5,3	70	7	0,7	0,07	0,007
99,9900%	5,2	100	10	1,0	0,1	0,01
99,9850%	5,1	150	15	1,5	0,15	0,015
99,9770%	5,0	230	23	2,3	0,23	0,023
99,9670%	4,9	330	33	3,3	0,33	0,033
99,9520%	4,8	480	48	4,8	0,48	0,048
99,9320%	4,7	680	68	6,8	0,68	0,068
99,9040%	4,6	960	96	9,6	0,96	0,096
99,8650%	4,5	1.350	135	13,5	1,35	0,135
99,8140%	4,4	1.860	186	18,6	1,86	0,186
99,7450%	4,3	2.550	255	25,5	2,55	0,255
99,6540%	4,2	3.460	346	34,6	3,46	0,346
99,5340%	4,1	4.660	466	46,6	4,66	0,466
99,3790%	4,0	6.210	621	62,1	6,21	0,621
99,1810%	3,9	8.190	819	81,9	8,19	0,819
98,930%	3,8	10.700	1.070	107	10,7	1,07
98,610%	3,7	13.900	1.390	139	13,9	1,39
98,220%	3,6	17.800	1.780	178	17,8	1,78
97,730%	3,5	22.700	2.270	227	22,7	2,27
97,130%	3,4	28.700	2.870	287	28,7	2,87
96,410%	3,3	35.900	3.590	359	35,9	3,59
95,540%	3,2	44.600	4.460	446	44,6	4,46
94,520%	3,1	54.800	5.480	548	54,8	5,48
93,320%	3,0	66.800	6.680	668	66,8	6,68
91,920%	2,9	80.800	8.080	808	80,8	8,08
90,320%	2,8	96.800	9.680	968	96,8	9,68
88,50%	2,7	115.000	11.500	1.150	115	11,5
86,50%	2,6	135.000	13.500	1.350	135	13,5
84,20%	2,5	158.000	15.800	1.580	158	15,8
81,60%	2,4	184.000	18.400	1.840	184	18,4
78,80%	2,3	212.000	21.200	2.120	212	21,2
76,80%	2,2	242.000	24.200	2.420	242	24,2
72,60%	2,1	274.000	27.400	2.740	274	27,4
69,20%	2,0	308.000	30.800	3.080	308	30,8
65,60%	1,9	344.000	34.400	3.440	344	34,4
61,80%	1,8	382.000	38.200	3.820	382	38,2
58,00%	1,7	420.000	42.000	4.200	420	42
54,00%	1,6	460.000	46.000	4.600	460	46
50,00%	1,5	500.000	50.000	5.000	500	50
46,00%	1,4	540.000	54.000	5.400	540	54
43,00%	1,3	570.000	57.000	5.700	570	57
39,00%	1,2	610.000	61.000	6.100	610	61
35,00%	1,1	650.000	65.000	6.500	650	65
31,00%	1,0	690.000	69.000	6.900	690	69
28,00%	0,9	720.000	72.000	7.200	720	72
25,00%	0,8	750.000	75.000	7.500	750	75
22,00%	0,7	780.000	78.000	7.800	780	78
19,00%	0,6	810.000	81.000	8.100	810	81
16,00%	0,5	840.000	84.000	8.400	840	84
14,00%	0,4	860.000	86.000	8.600	860	86
12,00%	0,3	880.000	88.000	8.800	880	88
10,00%	0,2	900.000	90.000	9.000	900	90
8,00%	0,1	920.000	92.000	9.200	920	92

Note: Subtract 1.5 to obtain the "long-term Sigma".

Printing: Krips bv, Meppel, The Netherlands
Binding: Stürtz, Würzburg, Germany

TRIZ Contradiction Matrix

Impr
1. W
2. W
3. Le
4. Le
5. Ar
6. Ar
7. Vo
8. Vo
9. Sp
10. F
11. S
12. S
13. S
14. S
15. D
16. D
17. T
18. I
19. E
20. E
21. F
22. U
23. U
24. U
25. U
26. C
27. I
28. I
29. I
30. I
31. I
32. I
33. I
34. I
35. A
36. C
37. C
38. I
39. I